Mike Bar

Love, Love

Methuen Drama

Published by Methuen Drama 2012

Methuen Drama, an imprint of Bloomsbury Publishing Plc

5 7 9 10 8 6 4

Methuen Drama
Bloomsbury Publishing Plc
50 Bedford Square
London WC1B 3DP
www.methuendrama.com

Copyright © Mike Bartlett 2010

Reprinted with amendments to the text in 2011
And with further amendments in 2012

Mike Bartlett has asserted his rights under the Copyright, Designs
and Patents Act 1988 to be identified as the author of this work

ISBN: 978 1 408 14063 5

A CIP catalogue record for this book is
available from the British Library

Available in the USA from Bloomsbury Academic & Professional,
175 Fifth Avenue/3rd Floor, New York, NY 10010.
www.BloomsburyAcademicUSA.com

Typeset by Mark Heslington Ltd, Scarborough, North Yorkshire
Printed and bound in the UK by The MPG Books Group, Bodmin, Cornwall

Caution

All rights whatsoever in this play are strictly reserved and application for
performance etc. should be made before rehearsals begin for professional
productions to The Agency (London) Ltd, 24 Pottery Lane, London
W11 4LZ and for English Language amateur productions outside the
United States of America and Canada to Performing Rights Manager,
Nick Hern Books Ltd, 14 Larden Road, London W3 7ST
(info@nickhernbooks.demon.co.uk). No performance may be
given unless a licence has been obtained.

No rights in incidental music or songs contained in the Work are hereby
granted and performance rights for any performance/presentation
whatsoever must be obtained from the respective copyright owners.

All rights reserved. No part of this publication may be reproduced in
any form or by any means – graphic, electronic or mechanical, including
photocopying, recording, taping or information storage and retrieval
systems – without the written permission of Bloomsbury Publishing Plc.

This book is produced using paper that is made from wood grown in
managed, sustainable forests. It is natural, renewable and recyclable.
The logging and manufacturing processes conform to the environmental
regulations of the country of origin.

ROYAL COURT

The Royal Court Theatre & Paines Plough in association with Drum Theatre Plymouth present

LOVE, LOVE, LOVE
by **Mike Bartlett**

Love, Love, Love was originally commissioned and co-produced by Paines Plough and the Drum Theatre Plymouth. It was first performed on 7 October 2010 at the Drum Theatre Plymouth with the following cast: Daniela Denby-Ashe (Sandra), James Barrett (Jamie), Simon Darwen (Henry), John Heffernan (Kenneth) and Rosie Wyatt (Rose).

The play retoured in 2011 for 14 weeks and the roles of Kenneth and Sandra were played by Ben Addis and Lisa Jackson.

Lighting was originally created by Hartley T A Kemp.

Principal Sponsor

LOVE, LOVE, LOVE

by Mike Bartlett

Kenneth **Ben Miles**
Henry **Sam Troughton**
Sandra **Victoria Hamilton**
Jamie **George Rainsford**
Rose **Claire Foy**

Director **James Grieve**
Designer **Lucy Osborne**
Lighting Designer **James Farncombe**
Sound Designer **Tom Gibbons**
Casting Director **Amy Ball**
Assistant Director **Caitlin McLeod**
Production Manager **Paul Handley**
Stage Manager **Alison Rich**
Deputy Stage Manager **Sarah Caselton-Smith**
Assistant Stage Manager **Adam McElderry**
Stage Management Work Placement **Laura Cunnick**
Costume Supervisor **Jackie Orton**
Hair & Make-Up **Carole Hancock & Michael Ward**
Wigs **Hum Studios**
Movement Director **Imogen Knight**
Dialect Coach **Michaela Kennen**
Set Builders **Miraculous Engineering**
Scenic Painter **Kerry Jarrett**

The Royal Court and Stage Management wish to thank the following for their help with this production: MacKing, Almeida Theatre, Tricycle Theatre, Donmar Warehouse, National Youth Theatre, English Touring Theatre, Young Vic, Haggle Vinyl, British Heart Foundation, Sebastian Bailey, Laura Cunnick, AJW Props, Paines Plough, Oxfam Bookstore, Honeyrose, Restore, Mark Russi and O2.

THE COMPANY

MIKE BARTLETT (Writer)

Mike is currently Associate Playwright at Paines Plough. In 2011 he was Writer-In-Residence at the National Theatre, and in 2007 he was Pearson Playwright in Residence at The Royal Court Theatre.

FOR THE ROYAL COURT: Cock, Contractions, My Child.

OTHER THEATRE INCLUDES: Love, Love, Love (Paines Plough/Theatre Royal Plymouth/UK Tour); 13 (National); Decade (Headlong); Earthquakes in London (Headlong/National/UK Tour); Artefacts (nabokov/Bush/59E59 Theatre).

RADIO INCLUDES: The Core, Heart, Liam, The Steps, Love Contract, Not Talking.

AS A THEATRE DIRECTOR: Honest (Royal & Derngate).

AWARDS INCLUDE: 2011 Theatre Award UK for Best New Play for Love, Love, Love; 2010 Olivier Award for Outstanding Acheivement in an Affiliate Theatre for Cock.

JAMES FARNCOMBE (Lighting Designer)

FOR THE ROYAL COURT: The Village Bike.

THEATRE INCLUDES: Juno and the Paycock (National/Gate Theatre, Dublin); Men Should Weep, Double Feature (National); The Duchess of Malfi (Old Vic); The Recruiting Officer, Inadmissible Evidence (Donmar); The Ladykillers (Liverpool Playhouse/West End); Ghost Stories (Liverpool Playhouse/Lyric Hammersmith/West End/Toronto); The Changeling, The Glass Menagerie (Young Vic); Swallows and Amazons (West End); Juliet and Her Romeo, Far Away (Bristol Old Vic); Lord of the Flies (Regent's Park); Twisted Tales (Lyric Hammersmith) Love, Love, Love (Paines Plough/Theatre Royal Plymouth/UK Tour); Plenty (Sheffield Crucible); Dancing at Lughnasa (Birmingham Rep); Like a Fishbone, The Whiskey Taster, 2000 Feet Away (Bush); The Overcoat (Gecko); Breaking the Silence (Nottingham Playhouse); Osama the Hero, Single Act (Hampstead).

web.mac.com/jamesfarncombe

CLAIRE FOY (Rose)

THEATRE INCLUDES: DNA, The Miracle, Baby Girl (National).

TELEVISION INCLUDES: Hacks, White Heat, The Night Watch, Upstairs Downstairs, The Promise, Going Postal, Pulse, Little Dorrit, Being Human.

FILM INCLUDES: Wreckers, Season of the Witch.

TOM GIBBONS (Sound Designer)

Tom trained at Central School of Speech and Drama and is resident Sound Designer for the international physical theatre company Parrot{in the}Tank.

THEATRE INCLUDES: Chalet Lines (Bush); Shivered (Southwark Playhouse); Romeo and Juliet (Headlong); Island (National/UK Tour); Disco Pigs (Young Vic); Dead Heavy Fantastic (Liverpool Everyman); Plenty (Crucible Studio); Encourage The Others (Almeida); Wasted (Paines Plough/UK Tour); Love, Love, Love (Paines Plough/Theatre Royal Plymouth/UK Tour); Faith, Hope and Charity, The Hostage, Toad, Present Tense (Southwark Playhouse); Sold (503); The Chairs (Ustinov Bath); The Country, The Road To Mecca, The Roman Bath, 1936, The Shawl (Arcola); The Knowledge, Little Platoons, 50 Ways To Leave Your Lover, 50 Ways To Leave Your Lover@Xmas, Broken Space Season (Bush); Bagpuss, Everything Must Go, Soho Streets (Soho); The Machine Gunners (Polka); Holes (New Wimbledon Studio); Terror Tales (Hampstead Studio); Faustus (Watford Palace/UK Tour); Faithless Bitches (Courtyard); FAT (Oval House/UK Tour); Just Me Bell (Graeae/UK Tour); Fanta Orange, Blue Heaven (Finborough).

AS ASSOCIATE SOUND DESIGNER: The Aliens (Bush Theatre).

JAMES GRIEVE (Director)

James is co-Artistic Director of Paines Plough. He was formerly Founder and Artistic Director of nabokov, and Associate Director of The Bush.

THEATRE INCLUDES: Love, Love, Love (Paines Plough/Theatre Royal Plymouth/UK Tour); Fly Me To The Moon, Tiny Volcanoes, Wasted, You Cannot Go Forward From Where You Are Right Now, The Sound of Heavy Rain (Paines Plough); A Nobody, The Whisky Taster, St Petersburg, Psychogeography (Bush); Artefacts (nabakov/The Bush/UK Tour/59E59 Theatre).

VICTORIA HAMILTON (Sandra)

THEATRE INCLUDES: Twelfth Night (Donmar West End); Once in a Lifetime, Summer Folk, Money (National); Suddenly Last Summer (Donmar/UK Tour); Sweet Panic (West End); A Day in the Death of Joe Egg (West End/Roundabout, NY); Home & Beauty (BKL); The Country Wife (Sheffield Crucible); As You Like It (Sheffield Crucible/Lyric Hammersmith); The Doctor's Dilemma (Almeida); King Lear, The Provoked Wife, The Seagull (Old Vic); Troilus and Cressida, As You Like It (RSC); The Master Builder (UK Tour/West End); Retreat, Memorandum (Orange Tree).

TELEVISION INCLUDES: Toast, Larkrise to Candleford, Time of Your Life, Trial & Retribution, Wide Sargasso Sea, The Shell Seekers, A Very Social Secretary, Jericho, Spine Chillers, To the Ends of the Earth, Goodbye Mr Chips, Baby Father I & II, Victoria & Albert, The Savages, Midsomer Murders, King Lear, The Merchant of Venice, Persuasion, Pride & Prejudice.

FILM INCLUDES: French Film, Scoop, Before You Go, Mansfield Park.

AWARDS INCLUDE: 2004 Critics Circle Award for Best Actress for Suddenly Last Summer; 2003 Evening Standard Award for Best Actress for Suddenly Last Summer; 2003 Critics Circle Award for Outstanding Broadway Debut for A Day in the Death of Joe Egg; 2000 Critics Circle Award for Best Actress for As You Like It; 1996 Critics Circle Award for Best Newcomer for The Master Builder.

CAITLIN MCLEOD (Assistant Director)

AS ASSISTANT DIRECTOR FOR THE ROYAL COURT: In Basildon, Haunted Child.

OTHER THEATRE DIRECTION INCLUDES: And I And Silence, Northern Star (Finborough); Slaughter City (RSC, rehearsed reading); The Lady's Not For Burning, Elephant's Graveyard (Warwick Arts Centre Studio); Seven Jewish Children (Capital Centre).

OTHER ASSISTANT DIRECTON INCLUDES: Hamlet (Globe); The Talented Mr Ripley (Northampton Theatre Royal); Touched (North Wall Theatre, Oxford).

Caitlin is the Trainee Director at the Royal Court.

BEN MILES (Kenneth)

FOR THE ROYAL COURT: My Child.

OTHER THEATRE INCLUDES: Betrayal (West End); Measure For Measure (Almeida); The Norman Conquests (Old Vic/Broadway); Richard II (Old Vic); Hand in Hand to the Promised Land (Hampstead); The Cherry Orchard, The London Cuckolds, Mary Stuart, Macbeth, Trelawny of the Wells, Fuente Ovejuna (National); The Tower (Almeida); The Miser (Chichester/Theatre Royal Haymarket); Two Gentlemen of Verona, Hamlet, Romeo and Juliet, Have, Ispanka (RSC); Winter's Tale (Young Vic); The Tempest (Phoebus Cart).

TELEVISION INCLUDES: The Suspicions of Mr Whicher, Zen, The Promise, Trial and Retribution, Lark Rise to Candleford, Sex, The City and Me, Freezing, Sea of Souls, Bon Voyage, After Thomas, Under the Greenwood Tree, Mr Harvey Lights A Candle, Spin, A Thing Called Love, Prime Suspect, The Project, The Forsythe Saga, Cold Feet, Coupling.

FILM INCLUDES: Five Years, Ninja Assassin, Speed Racer, V For Vendetta, Imagine Me & You, Three Blind Mice, Love Again, Affair of the Necklace, Keep the Asperdistra Flying, Wings of the Dove.

LUCY OSBORNE (Designer)

Lucy graduated from Motley Theatre Design School, having also gained a BA in Fine Art from the University of Newcastle. Lucy was an Associate Artist at the Bush Theatre.
FOR THE ROYAL COURT: Shades.
THEATRE INCLUDES: Love, Love, Love (Paines Plough/Theatre Royal Plymouth/UK Tour); The Recruiting Officer (Donmar); Blue Heart Afternoon (Hampstead); The Roundabout Season (Paines Plough/Sheffield Crucible); Huis Clos (Donmar); The Taming of the Shrew, Twelfth Night (Chicago Shakespeare Theatre); Plenty, The Long and the Short and The Tall, The Unthinkable (Sheffield Crucible); Precious Little Talent (West End); Where's My Seat, The Aliens, Like a Fishbone, The Whisky Taster, If There Is I Haven't Found It Yet, Wrecks, Broken Space Festival, Sea Wall, 2,000 Feet Away, Tinderbox, tHe dYsFUnCKshOnalZ! (Bush).
TELEVISION INCLUDES: Here, When Romeo Met Juliet.
AWARDS INCLUDE: Jeff Award for Theatre Design.

GEORGE RAINSFORD (Jamie)

THEATRE INCLUDES: Roald Dahl's Twisted Tales (Lyric Hammersmith/Liverpool Playhouse); The Man, Men Without Shadows (Finborough); Days of Significance (RSC); All's Well That End's Well (National); Polar Bear (Birmingham Rep); Chatroom/Citizenship (National/UK Tour/Hong Kong Arts Festival); The Three Musketeers (Bristol Old Vic); The 24 Hour Plays (Old Vic).
TELEVISION INCLUDES: Casualty, Call the Midwife, Law & Order: UK, Secret Diary of a Call Girl, Waking the Dead, Doctors, Panorama: A Good Kicking.
FILM INCLUDES: Wild Target, Souvenirs.

SAM TROUGHTON (Henry)

THEATRE INCLUDES: A Streetcar Named Desire (Liverpool Playhouse); Morte D'Arthur, Romeo and Juliet, The Grain Store, Julius Caesar, The Winter's Tale, A Midsummer Night's Dream, Richard III, Henry VI Part I, II & III, The Taming of the Shrew (RSC); An Oak Tree (Birmingham Rep); As You Like It (Sheffield Crucible); Nathan the Wise (Hampstead); Buried Child, The Coast of Utopia, Tartuffe (National); School for Scandal (Derby/Northampton); A Midsummer Night's Dream (Canizaro Park); The Other Shore (Attic Theatre Co.); Hamlet (Orange Tree).
TELEVISION INCLUDES: Silent Witness, Robin Hood, Hex II, Messiah III, Gunpowder, Treason and Plot, Judge John Deed, Seven Wonders of the Industrial Age, Ultimate Force, Blue Dove, Foyle's War, Summer in the Suburbs.
FILM INCLUDES: Spirit Trap, Alien vs Predator, Vera Drake, Sylvia.

THE RIOT CLUB HITS THE WEST END
11 MAY - 4 AUGUST 2012

A PLAY BY
LAURA WADE

DUKE OF YORK'S THEATRE • ST. MARTIN'S LANE, LONDON WC2N 4GB
PHONE: 08448717623 • ROYAL COURT THEATRE BOX OFFICE: 02075655000
POSHTHEPLAY.COM

THE ENGLISH STAGE COMPANY AT THE ROYAL COURT THEATRE

'For me the theatre is really a religion or way of life. You must decide what you feel the world is about and what you want to say about it, so that everything in the theatre you work in is saying the same thing ... A theatre must have a recognisable attitude. It will have one, whether you like it or not.'

George Devine, first artistic director of the English Stage Company: notes for an unwritten book.

photo: Stephen Cummiskey

As Britain's leading national company dedicated to new work, the Royal Court Theatre produces new plays of the highest quality, working with writers from all backgrounds, and addressing the problems and possibilities of our time.

"The Royal Court has been at the centre of British cultural life for the past 50 years, an engine room for new writing and constantly transforming the theatrical culture." Stephen Daldry

Since its foundation in 1956, the Royal Court has presented premieres by almost every leading contemporary British playwright, from John Osborne's Look Back in Anger to Caryl Churchill's A Number and Tom Stoppard's Rock 'n' Roll. Just some of the other writers to have chosen the Royal Court to premiere their work include Edward Albee, John Arden, Richard Bean, Samuel Beckett, Edward Bond, Leo Butler, Jez Butterworth, Martin Crimp, Ariel Dorfman, Stella Feehily, Christopher Hampton, David Hare, Eugène Ionesco, Ann Jellicoe, Terry Johnson, Sarah Kane, David Mamet, Martin McDonagh, Conor McPherson, Joe Penhall, Lucy Prebble, Mark Ravenhill, Simon Stephens, Wole Soyinka, Polly Stenham, David Storey, Debbie Tucker Green, Arnold Wesker and Roy Williams.

"It is risky to miss a production there." Financial Times

In addition to its full-scale productions, the Royal Court also facilitates international work at a grass roots level, developing exchanges which bring young writers to Britain and sending British writers, actors and directors to work with artists around the world. The research and play development arm of the Royal Court Theatre, The Studio, finds the most exciting and diverse range of new voices in the UK. The Studio runs play-writing groups including the Young Writers Programme, Critical Mass for black, Asian and minority ethnic writers and the biennial Young Writers Festival. For further information, go to www.royalcourttheatre.com/playwriting/the-studio.

"Yes, the Royal Court is on a roll. Yes, Dominic Cooke has just the genius and kick that this venue needs... It's fist-bitingly exciting." Independent

∞ Paines Plough

"A major force for new writing" *The Guardian*

Paines Plough is the UK's national theatre of new plays. The company commission and produce the best playwrights and tour their plays far and wide. Whether you're in Liverpool or Lyme Regis, Scarborough or Southampton, a Paines Plough show is coming to a theatre near you soon.

Paines Plough was founded in 1974 over a pint of Paines bitter in the Plough pub. Since then they have produced more than 100 new productions by world renowned playwrights like Stephen Jeffreys, Abi Morgan, Sarah Kane, Mark Ravenhill, Dennis Kelly and Mike Bartlett. Those plays have all been toured to hundreds of places from Manchester to Moscow to Maidenhead.

"Paines Plough has hit new heights since Grieve and Perrin took over as artistic directors. The company's output has been astonishing." *The Stage*

At Paines Plough

Artistic Directors	**James Grieve**
	George Perrin
Producer	**Tara Wilkinson**
General Manager	**Claire Simpson**
Assistant Producer (WASTED)	**Hanna Streeter**
Interim Administrator	**Sean Linnen**
Production Manager	**Bernd Fauler**
Production Assistant (Stage One)	**Sarah Stribley**
Admin Intern	**Stephanie Königer**
Press Representative	**Kate Morley***
*denotes freelance	

Board of Directors
Ola Animashawun, Christopher Bath, Tamara Cizeika, Marilyn Imrie, Nia Janis, Zarine Kharas, Caro Newling (Chair), Simon Stephens

Contact
Paines Plough,
  4th Floor, 43 Aldwych, London, WC2B 4DN
T +44 (0) 20 7240 4533 fax +44 (0) 20 7240 4534
office@painesplough.com
www.painesplough.com

Follow @PainesPlough on Twitter
Add Paines Plough on Facebook
Sign up to our newsletter at
www.painesplough.com

The Roundabout Auditorium

We're creating the UK's first portable small-scale in-the-round touring amphitheatre. We're calling it **The Roundabout Auditorium**. Our aim is to make the best contemporary plays available to everyone, irrespective of geography, in high quality productions and in an exciting 360° experience.

To help us build our dream theatre: **www.justgiving.com/painesplough**

PLYMOUTH THEATRES

"Geography still everything in British theatre. If the Drum Plymouth was in London it would be feted as it deserves"
Lyn Gardner via Twitter

The Theatre Royal Plymouth is the largest and best attended regional producing theatre in the UK and the leading promoter of theatre in the South West. There are two distinctive performance spaces; the Theatre Royal and the Drum Theatre, as well as TR2, an award-winning theatre production and education centre containing unrivalled set, costume, prop-making and rehearsal facilities.

The Drum Theatre produces and presents new plays. It has built a national reputation for the quality of its programme and innovative work, winning the prestigious Peter Brook Empty Space Award. As well producing its own plays, the Drum Theatre regularly collaborates with leading theatres and companies in the UK.

"Plymouth's Drum is a real powerhouse of innovative theatre and collaboration"
The Guardian

Our recent productions include:
The Empire by DC Moore in co-production with The Royal Court
Teenage Riot with Ontroerend Goed
Love, Love, Love by Mike Bartlett with Paines Plough
Chekhov in Hell by Dan Rebellato
And the Horse You Rode In On with Told by an Idiot
The Golden Dragon by Roland Schimmelpfennig with ATC
Lovesong by Abi Morgan with Frantic Assembly
Audience with Ontroerend Goed
Keep Breathing by Chris Goode
Horse Piss For Blood by Carl Grose
A History of Everything with Ontroerend Goed

  Supported by
ARTS COUNCIL ENGLAND

ROYAL COURT SUPPORTERS

The Royal Court is able to offer its unique playwriting and audience development programmes because of significant and longstanding partnerships with the organisations that support it.

Coutts is the Principal Sponsor of the Royal Court. The Genesis Foundation supports the Royal Court's work with International Playwrights. Theatre Local is sponsored by Bloomberg. The Jerwood Charitable Foundation supports new plays by playwrights through the Jerwood New Playwrights series. The Andrew Lloyd Webber Foundation supports the Royal Court's Studio, which aims to seek out, nurture and support emerging playwrights. Over the past ten years the BBC has supported the Gerald Chapman Fund for directors.

The Harold Pinter Playwright's Award is given annually by his widow, Lady Antonia Fraser, to support a new commission at the Royal Court.

PUBLIC FUNDING
Arts Council England, London
British Council
European Commission Representation in the UK

CHARITABLE DONATIONS
American Friends of the Royal Court Theatre
Martin Bowley Charitable Trust
Gerald Chapman Fund
City Bridge Trust
Cowley Charitable Trust
The Dorset Foundation
The John Ellerman Foundation
The Eranda Foundation
Genesis Foundation
J Paul Getty Jnr Charitable Trust
The Golden Bottle Trust
The Haberdashers' Company
Paul Hamlyn Foundation
Jerwood Charitable Foundation
Marina Kleinwort Charitable Trust
The Leathersellers' Company
The Andrew Lloyd Webber Foundation
John Lyon's Charity
The Andrew W Mellon Foundation
The David & Elaine Potter Foundation
Rose Foundation
Royal Victoria Hall Foundation
The Dr Mortimer & Theresa Sackler Foundation
John Thaw Foundation
The Vandervell Foundation
The Garfield Weston Foundation

CORPORATE SUPPORTERS & SPONSORS
BBC
Bloomberg
Coutts
Ecosse Films
Kudos Film & Television
MAC
Moët & Chandon
Oakley Capital Limited
Smythson of Bond Street
White Light Ltd

BUSINESS ASSOCIATES, MEMBERS & BENEFACTORS
Auerbach & Steele Opticians
Bank of America Merrill Lynch
Hugo Boss
Lazard
Louis Vuitton
Oberon Books
Peter Jones
Savills
Vanity Fair

DEVELOPMENT ADVOCATES
John Ayton MBE
Elizabeth Bandeen
Kinvara Balfour
Anthony Burton CBE
Piers Butler
Sindy Caplan
Sarah Chappatte
Cas Donald (Vice Chair)
Celeste Fenichel
Emma Marsh (Chair)
William Russell
Deborah Shaw Marquardt (Vice Chair)
Sian Westerman
Nick Wheeler
Daniel Winterfeldt

Supported by
ARTS COUNCIL ENGLAND

INDIVIDUAL MEMBERS

GROUND-BREAKERS

Anonymous
Moira Andreae
Mr & Mrs Simon Andrews
Nick Archdale
Charlotte Asprey
Jane Attias
Brian Balfour-Oatts
Elizabeth & Adam Bandeen
Ray Barrell
Dr Kate Best
Dianne & Michael Bienes
Stan & Val Bond
Kristina Borsy & Nick Turdean
Neil & Sarah Brener
Mrs Deborah Brett
Mrs Joanna Buckhenham
Clive & Helena Butler
Sindy & Jonathan Caplan
Gavin & Lesley Casey
Sarah & Philippe Chappatte
Christine Collins
Tim & Caroline Clark
Carole & Neville Conrad
Kay Ellen Consolver & John Storkerson
Anthony & Andrea Coombs
Clyde Cooper
Ian & Caroline Cormack
Mr & Mrs Cross
Andrew & Amanda Cryer
Alison Davies
Noel De Keyzer
Polly Devlin OBE
Glen Donovan
Denise & Randolph Dumas
Robyn Durie
Zeina Durra & Saadi Soudavar
Glenn & Phyllida Earle
Allie Esiri
Mark & Sarah Evans
Margaret Exley CBE
Celeste & Peter Fenichel
Margy Fenwick
John Garfield
Beverley Gee
Dina Geha & Eric Lopez

Mr & Mrs Georgiades
Nick & Julie Gould
Lord & Lady Grabiner
Richard & Marcia Grand
Reade & Elizabeth Griffith
Don & Sue Guiney
Jill Hackel & Andrzej Zarzycki
Carol Hall
Mary & Douglas Hampson
Sally Hampton
Jennifer Harper
Sam & Caroline Haubold
Anoushka Healy
Madeleine Hodgkin
Mr & Mrs Gordon Holmes
Damien Hyland
The David Hyman Charitable Trust
Amanda Ibbetson
Nicholas Jones
Nicholas Josefowitz
Dr Evi Kaplanis
David Kaskel & Christopher Teano
Vincent & Amanda Keaveny
Peter & Maria Kellner
Nicola Kerr
Diala & Tarek Khlat
Philip & Joan Kingsley
Mr & Mrs Pawel Kisielewski
Sarah & David Kowitz
Maria Lam
Rosemary Leith
Larry & Peggy Levy
Daisy & Richard Littler
Kathryn Ludlow
James & Beatrice Lupton
Dr Ekaterina Malievskaia & George Goldsmith
Christopher Marek Rencki
Barbara Minto
Ann & Gavin Neath CBE
Murray North
Clive & Annie Norton
Georgia Oetker
Mr & Mrs Guy Patterson
William Plapinger & Cassie Murray

Andrea & Hilary Ponti
Annie & Preben Prebensen
Julie Ritter
Mark & Tricia Robinson
Paul & Gill Robinson
Sir & Lady Ruddock
William & Hilary Russell
Julie & Bill Ryan
Sally & Anthony Salz
Bhags Sharma
The Michael & Melanie Sherwood Charitable Foundation
Tom Siebens & Mimi Parsons
Andy Simpkin
Richard Simpson
Paul & Rita Skinner
Mr & Mrs RAH Smart
Brian Smith
Samantha & Darren Smith
Mr Michael Spencer
Sue St Johns
The Ulrich Family
The Ury Trust
Amanda Vail
Constance Von Unruh
Ian & Victoria Watson
Matthew & Sian Westerman
Carol Woolton
Katherine & Michael Yates

BOUNDARY-BREAKERS

Katie Bradford
Sir Trevor & Lady Chinn
Leonie Fallstrom
Piers & Melanie Gibson
David Harding
Mr & Mrs Roderick Jack
Ms Alex Joffe
Steve Kingshott
Emma Marsh
Philippa Thorp
Mr & Mrs Nick Wheeler

MOVER-SHAKERS

Anonymous
Mr & Mrs Ayton MBE
Cas Donald
Lloyd & Sarah Dorfman
Lydia & Manfred Gorvy
Duncan Matthews QC
Ian & Carol Sellars
Edgar & Judith Wallner

HISTORY-MAKERS

Eric Abraham & Sigrid Rausing

MAJOR DONORS

Rob & Siri Cope
Daniel & Joanna Friel
Jack & Linda Keenan
Deborah & Stephen Marquardt
Miles Morland
NoraLee & Jon Sedmak
Jan & Michael Topham
Stuart & Hilary Williams Charitable Foundation

Thank you to all our Friends, Stage-Takers and Ice-Breakers for their generous support.

APPLAUDING
THE EXCEPTIONAL.

Coutts is proud to sponsor the Royal Court Theatre

FOR THE ROYAL COURT

Royal Court Theatre, Sloane Square, London SW1W 8AS
Tel: 020 7565 5050 Fax: 020 7565 5001
info@royalcourttheatre.com, www.royalcourttheatre.com

Artistic Director **Dominic Cooke**
Associate Directors **Simon Godwin, Jeremy Herrin*, Sacha Wares***
Artistic Associate **Emily McLaughlin***
Diversity Associate **Ola Animashawun***
Education Associate **Lynne Gagliano***
PA to the Artistic Director **Pamela Wilson**
Trainee Director **Caitlin Mcleod ‡**

Executive Director **Kate Horton**
General Manager **Catherine Thornborrow**
Administrative Assistant **Holly Handel**
Trainee Producer (funded by Stage One) **Daniel Brodie**

Literary Manager **Christopher Campbell**
Senior Reader **Nic Wass***
Studio Administrator **Clare McQuillan**
Studio Assistant **Tom Lyons***
Writers' Tutor **Leo Butler***
Pearson Playwright **DC Moore**

Associate Director International **Elyse Dodgson**
International Projects Manager **Chris James**
International Associate **Caroline Steinbeis**

Casting Director **Amy Ball**
Casting Assistant **Lotte Hines**

Head of Production **Paul Handley**
JTU Production Manager **Tariq Rifaat**
Production Assistant **Zoe Hurwitz**
Head of Lighting **Matt Drury**
Lighting Deputy **Stephen Andrews**
Lighting Assistants **Katie Pitt, Jack Williams**
Lighting Board Operator **Jack Champion**
Head of Stage **Steven Stickler**
Stage Deputy **Dan Lockett**
Stage Chargehand **Lee Crimmen**
Chargehand Carpenter **Richard Martin**
Head of Sound **David McSeveney**
Sound Deputy **Alex Caplen**
Sound Operator **Sam Charleston**
Head of Costume **Iona Kenrick**
Costume Deputy **Jackie Orton**
Wardrobe Assistant **Pam Anson**

ENGLISH STAGE COMPANY

President
Dame Joan Plowright CBE

Honorary Council
Sir Richard Eyre CBE
Alan Grieve CBE
Martin Paisner CBE

Council
Chairman **Anthony Burton CBE**
Vice Chairman **Graham Devlin CBE**

Head of Finance & Administration **Helen Perryer**
Finance Manager **Martin Wheeler**
Finance Officer **Rachel Harrison***
Finance & Administration Assistant (Maternity Leave) **Tessa Rivers**
Finance & Administration Assistant (Maternity Cover) **Rosie Mortimer**

Head of Marketing & Sales **Becky Wootton**
Marketing Manager **Ruth Waters**
Press & Public Relations Officer **Anna Evans**
Communications Officer **Ruth Hawkins**
Communications General Assistant **Jennie Eggleton**
Communications Intern **Alex Sayer**

Sales Manager **Kevin West**
Deputy Sales Manager **Liam Geoghegan**
Box Office Sales Assistants **Joe Hodgson, Carla Kingham*, Ciara O'Toole*, Helen Preddy, Chelsea Nelson, Stephen McGill*.**

Head of Development **Gaby Styles**
Senior Development Manager **Sue Livermore**
Development Managers **Lucy Buxton, Luciana Lawlor**
Development Officer **Penny Saward**
Development Intern **Abee McCallum**

Theatre Manager **Bobbie Stokes**
Front of House Manager **Rachel Dudley**
Front of House Assistant **Joe White**
Events Manager (Maternity Leave) **Joanna Ostrom**
Duty Managers **Fiona Clift*, Elinor Keber*, Mila Sanders***
Bar & Food Manager **Sami Rifaat**
Deputy Bar & Food Manager **Ali Christian**
Bar and Food Supervisor **TJ Chappell***
Head Chef **Tim Jenner**
Sous Chef **Paulino Chuitcheu**
Bookshop Manager **Simon David**
Bookshop Assistant **Vanessa Hammick***
Stage Door/Reception **Paul Lovegrove, Tyrone Lucas**

Thanks to all of our ushers and bar staff.

‡ The post of Trainee Director is supported by an anonymous donor.

This theatre has the support of the Pearson Playwrights' Scheme sponsored by the Peggy Ramsay Foundation.

* Part-time.

Members
Jennette Arnold OBE
Judy Daish
Sir David Green KCMG
Joyce Hytner OBE
Stephen Jeffreys
Wasfi Kani OBE
Phyllida Lloyd CBE
James Midgley
Sophie Okonedo OBE
Alan Rickman
Anita Scott
Katharine Viner
Lord Stewart Wood

Love, Love, Love

Characters

Kenneth
Henry
Sandra
Jamie
Rose

The play should take place in a proscenium arch theatre.
A red curtain should close between scenes.

(/) means the next speech begins at that point
(–) means the next line interrupts
(. . .) at the end of a speech means it trails off. On its own it indicates
a pressure, expectation or desire to speak.

A line with no full stop at the end indicates that the next speech
follows on immediately.

A speech with no written dialogue indicates a character deliberately
remaining silent.

One

Curtain up.

The sound of the Vienna Boys' Choir singing.

25 June 1967. A north London flat. It's a mess. Smoky. Unwashed glasses on table.

Kenneth *has the television on. He walks around wearing tweed trousers and a dressing gown. He comes out of the kitchen with a glass of brandy, puts it down on the side. Then moves back, runs and athletically jumps over the back of the sofa into the seat.*

He lights a cigarette.

Watches the television.

Relaxes.

Realises he's left his brandy on the side.

Tries to reach it from the sofa.

Really tries.

Gives up, gets up, gets the brandy and sits back down.

The door opens.

Henry *enters. His hair is neat – he wears a black leather jacket.*

Kenneth   You're late.

Henry   So?

Kenneth   You're missing the programme.

>   **Henry** *takes off his jacket. Underneath he wears a black cardigan, shirt and tie.*

Henry   What programme?

Kenneth   Look.

>   **Henry** *does, for a moment.*

Kenneth   Twenty-six countries are broadcasting this, right now. Across the world.

Thought you were interested.

Henry   Things to do, haven't I?

Kenneth   You said you'd be back for it.

Henry   I've been working all day. I have to pay rent. Don't get a free ride.

Kenneth   A free ride.

Henry   Not like some people.

Kenneth   You could go to university if you wanted.

Henry   Bit old for that now.

Kenneth   No. You're not –

Henry   Doesn't matter doesn't matter.

Kenneth   You're not too old you can get a grant, a scholarship you know.

Henry   Doesn't matter.

Kenneth   You might get one.

Even you.

Henry   Shut it.

He sits in an arm chair.

They watch for a moment.

Kenneth   This has never happened before in the history of mankind. Across the world four hundred million people, including us, are all watching this one thing at exactly the same time.

They keep watching. After a moment,

Henry   What's on the other side?

Kenneth	Henry, this isn't beyond you, this isn't a clever thing, this is for everyone, every single person across the world, you've got to understand the significance. It's America, Europe, Japan. It's twenty-six different countries, cultures and languages coming together. It's remarkable. It signifies a new age of international cooperation.
Henry	What are they showing then?
Kenneth	The Beatles.
Henry	That's not the Beatles.
Kenneth	Later on it will be.
Henry	Who's that?
Kenneth	The Vienna Boys' Choir.
Henry	The Vienna Boys' Choir?
Kenneth	Yeah.
Henry	Bloody hell.
Kenneth	I know, but if you –
Henry	Turn to the other side.
Kenneth	They illustrate the point, exactly what I'm saying, Austria chose a choir, Britain chose *the Beatles*. Out of everyone and anything in the whole country.

Henry *takes one of* **Kenneth**'s *cigarettes.*

Kenneth	It could've been politicians or old men, an orchestra or ballet or something old like that something old but it wasn't. It was pop music. Young people, like us dressed up as they want. Things are changing every day at the moment.

Henry *lights a cigarette.*

Henry	You been out at all?
Kenneth	Once or twice . . .

Henry   Right.

Kenneth   I got your beans.

Henry   What?

Kenneth   Your beans.

Henry

Kenneth   You said we needed beans.

Henry   What about bog paper?

Kenneth   Do we need . . .

Henry   Well there isn't any.

Kenneth   Really?

Henry   Is there?

Kenneth   I don't know.

Henry   Did you see any?

Kenneth   No but

Henry   Well then.

Kenneth   Thought you might have it hidden away.

Henry   Why would I –

Kenneth   Or something.

Henry   Hidden it?

Kenneth   Or something. Yeah.

          Beat.

Henry   What about butter, milk? You get any of that?

Kenneth   Thought it was just the beans you needed.

Henry   Just the beans . . .

Kenneth   Yeah just the beans. That's all you said to get, so
          that's what I got, following orders Henry, just
          following orders.

Henry   Perhaps you should go home. Maybe your time
              in my flat is coming to an end, I think you
              should pack up actually.

Kenneth   You're tired I can tell.

Henry   Yeah that's right Ken I am tired. Fucking
              knackered as it happens.

          Kenneth *goes and pours him a brandy.*

Henry   Dad called me today.

Kenneth   At work?

Henry   At work. On the telephone yes. Don't talk to
              him much like that. He speaks all properly,
              accentuates his vowels, like the queen or
              something.

Kenneth   He thinks people listen.

Henry   People?

Kenneth   Listen in. The government.

Henry   Really?

Kenneth   What he said.

Henry   He's a mad old man sometimes.

Kenneth   Something to do with the war I reckon.

Henry   Mad old bastard.

          A moment.

Kenneth   What did he want?

Henry   He said 'We were under the impression
              Kenneth was at Oxford over the summer'.
              Oh right, I said.

              'But when we tried to contact him it turns out
              he left at the end of term, got a lift somewhere,
              not a word from him . . . and then we receive
              this letter'

Kenneth   They got it then.

Henry   Mum thinks you've been kidnapped.

Kenneth   I said I was alright, that's the only reason I bothered, to reassure her –

Henry   She thinks they held you at gunpoint, forced you to write it.

Kenneth   They're insane, both of them.

Henry   You should call.

Kenneth   No.

Henry   You will. I have to put up with it otherwise. Telephone.

Kenneth   Hassle though.

Henry   Or go home, that's your other option Kenneth, you could just go back home.

Kenneth   No. It's always the same, when I'm away they moan, they say they miss me, but soon as I arrive, they ignore me.

Henry   They thought I might know something about your disappearance.

Kenneth   And you said?

Henry   I said you don't tell me anything.

Kenneth   Right.

Henry   Hadn't heard from you in ages.

Kenneth   Thanks. You're a brother, a real brother to me.

Henry   I also said I thought you were a layabout little sod, an ungrateful little runt, that you should give them some of that grant you've got, give it back to them both.

Kenneth   Is that what you think?

Henry	You're making as much as Dad and he works like a dog.
Kenneth	I'm the future of this country,
Henry	My bloody taxes.
Kenneth	It's an investment.

Beat.

I appreciate you taking me in, Henry.

I needed to get away.

You know, break out for a bit, like.

The thought of spending all those weeks stuck in that house middle of nowhere, with Mum and Dad, can't drink, can't smoke, nowhere to go, nothing, absolutely nothing to do, it's like . . .

Like a prison sentence or something.

Henry	You could get a job.
Kenneth	We're not supposed to get a job, suppose to concentrate on our studies. I don't need a job anyway got my grant so –
Henry	That's right you don't need a job you've got your *grant*.

What about your friends, your lot from school, they're still around, must be.

Kenneth	They're just as bad, they're small, nothing. I needed somewhere exciting. I'm not being arrogant, but you understand, you moved away.
Henry	Yeah well . . .
Kenneth	You came to where things are happening. You don't just hear about things in London, or read them in the papers, you see them, you're on the spot. It's the Post Office Tower, the river, the

Stones, the Beatles – exhibitions, fashion, the cars, the *birds*.

Henry   The birds are something yes.

Kenneth   Even bloody Harold Wilson. Saw him the other day. He's smaller than you'd think.

Henry *gets up and switches the TV off.*

Kenneth   Oi. I was watching that.

Henry   No you weren't.

Kenneth   It's important.

Henry   It's a *choir*.

Beat.

So what you doing tonight?

Out somewhere?

Off out I presume?

Kenneth   No.

Henry   You're not?

Kenneth   Thought I'd watch television actually.

Henry   Said you wanted excitement. You could watch television at home.

Kenneth   No.

Henry   Why not?

Kenneth   Mum and Dad don't have one.

Henry   Yes they do, in the corner.

Kenneth   It blew up during the football.

Henry   What?

Kenneth   The World Cup. Didn't you notice?

Henry   Haven't been home for a while.

Kenneth	After that they said it was a waste of time and money getting another, said they'd rather listen to the radio.

Pause.

Henry	Plenty of skirt out there.
Kenneth	Yeah.
Henry	Plenty of birds.
Kenneth	Right.
Henry	Haven't you got a chum or something, someone you could meet?
Kenneth	You want me out.
Henry	Well not to put too fine a point on it.
Kenneth	What's her name?
Henry	None of your business actually though is it Kenneth?

Pause.

Kenneth	I'm settled now.
Henry	You're *settled*.
Kenneth	Got my brandy and fags, my house coat.
Henry	Is that what it is?
Kenneth	Yeah.
Henry	Thought you were ill or something.
Kenneth	Bloke at Oxford gave it to me.
Henry	A present?
Kenneth	Yeah.
Henry	Poof is he?
Kenneth	What?
Henry	Was he a poof?

Kenneth   Don't think so.

Henry   Are you?

Kenneth   What?

Henry   A bender.

Kenneth   Hard to say isn't it?

Henry   Is it?

Kenneth   What?

Henry   Are you a poof?

Kenneth   No.

Henry   You look like one.

Kenneth   Do I?

Henry   In that. Look like a proper queer.

Kenneth   Nothing wrong with being queer.

Henry   You are then.

Kenneth   No, but there's nothing wrong with it.

Henry   Fucking Oxford, look at you.

Kenneth   Henry.

Henry

Kenneth   Nothing like this has ever happened before.
The laws are constantly being overthrown,
the boundaries of what's possible, the music's
exploding, the walls collapsing. That's what's
going on. That's what's changing. We travel,
do what we want, wear what we like. Enjoy it.
Experiment.

We're breaking free.

Henry   Well you can break free right now and bugger
off she'll be here in a minute.

Kenneth   No.

Henry   Yes.

Kenneth   I don't have any money.

Henry   . . .

Beat.

Kenneth   I won't be in the way.

Henry   You will be in the way.

Kenneth   She could bring a friend.

Henry   I don't reckon she could actually Kenneth.

Kenneth   Make up a four.

Henry   No.

Kenneth   Never done that have we, brothers with birds, the McLarens used to walk down the street, you remember, down the street, they used to wear jackets, looked the same, like just the two of them, there's strength in brothers, we've never done that. Do you remember the McLarens? Birds used to lap that up the two of them next to each other, birds used to love it.

I heard a story once about them, they were in this club, one of those places they used to go to, and this bunch of totty comes up to them and says we're going to make your day and they went back to their house and all the girls lined up, and the McLarens picked teams like football teams, till there were like five-a-side, then they took their side up to their room, and . . . well I don't know what they did. All that she said – Frank Jameson's sister Tracey, she was one of the girls –– all she said was she had a great time.

A great time.

Do you ever feel you're missing out Henry?

Not saying we'd do that, but it makes you think we might be missing a trick.

Henry *has taken some money out of his wallet – offers it to* **Kenneth**.

Kenneth   What?

Henry   Here's a few bob, now fuck off.

Kenneth   No come on.

Henry   Bit deaf tonight Kenneth are you?

Kenneth   What's her name?

He slaps **Kenneth** *round the head, not hard, but enough. Then puts the money in* **Kenneth**'s *hand.*

Kenneth   She has got a name?

Henry   Course she's got a name.

Kenneth   What?

Henry   You remember the fights we had?

Kenneth   What is it?

Henry   You remember the fights?

Kenneth   Course I do.

He keeps his distance.

You always won I know that, I don't want to fight you I just want to know her name, won't make any difference, will it, you telling me, just saying what she's called, will it? Will it?

Henry   Sandra.

Kenneth   Good name. Sandra.

Henry   Yeah.

Kenneth   You and her been doing it long then?

Henry   We're not doing it.

Kenneth	Oh right not doing it.
Henry	Not yet, not so far. First time she's come round. Big moment you see? So I don't want some spotty bastard cluttering up the place, wearing his queer fucking coat of many colours.

You understand.

So.

Piss. Off.

Beat.

Kenneth	You're going to let her see it like this?
Henry	What?
Kenneth	The flat.
Henry	It's alright.
Kenneth	You let her see it like this, she'll run a mile turn right round off she'll go.
Henry	
Kenneth	
Henry	It was alright before you arrived.
Kenneth	Come on.

I'll help.

I'll help you tidy.

Henry *doesn't move.*

Kenneth	Come on.

I will, I'll help, then I'll go.

Promise.

They tidy.

Henry*'s efficient at it.*

Kenneth *is slapdash.*

Kenneth   Is she pretty?

Henry   Yeah.

    Beat.

      Beautiful.

    They tidy.

Kenneth   Clever?

Henry   Yeah.

Kenneth   Legs?

Henry   Up to here.

Kenneth   Up to where?

Henry   Where do you think?

Kenneth   Nice figure then.

Henry   She's a piece of work all round, I'm telling you.

Kenneth   Classy?

Henry   Bit posh yeah.

Kenneth   Yeah.

Henry   Middle class, you know, dresses up nice, every
               time I've seen her she's nice looking. Makes an
               effort, hair, and the face. You know. She's into all
               that anti-nuclear wotnot, and women. Talks a lot
               about women. She goes to groups. Protests.

Kenneth   Where?

Henry   University I think.

Kenneth   She's a student.

Henry   Yeah. She's political. All that.

Kenneth   Thought you didn't like political women.

Henry   I don't.

Kenneth   Right.

Henry   But you should see her knockers.

Kenneth   Henry –

Henry   Bloody marvellous. Size of footballs. More than makes up for the political nonsense she comes out with.

Kenneth   You said that to her?

Henry   Might've mentioned it yeah.

Kenneth   What did she say?

Henry   That I was a chauvinist.

Kenneth   Bit unfair.

Henry   I know. I told her, I'm not driving anyone around, they can drive themselves.

Kenneth   That's not what chauvinist means.

Henry   Bloody hell Kenneth you really think I'm a fucking thick bastard don't you?

       Beat.

       I know what it means.

       Maybe I didn't go to Oxford University, but I'm not a bloody – no no don't leave those there.

       Henry *takes some dishes* **Kenneth** *has put in a cupboard and takes them through to the kitchen.*

Kenneth   What time's she getting here?

Henry   Nine o clock. What time is it now?

Kenneth   Ten to.

Henry   You going to bugger off then?

Kenneth   Yeah, I'll finish this, then go off to my room.

Henry   Your room?

Kenneth   Leave you to it.

Henry   You're not going in your room, you're
going out.

Kenneth   Got books to read I'll be fine.

Henry   You're going to stay in there all night?

Kenneth   They're long books lots of words you know me
I'll be fine.

Beat.

Henry   Alright. But you better stay shut up in there. I'm
telling you.

Kenneth   I will.

Henry   Even if you want a piss. You do it out the
window or something. In a bucket. Whatever.
You stay put.

Kenneth   Alright.

Henry   Understand?

Kenneth   Yeah.

They tidy.

Do you talk to him much then?

Henry   Who?

Kenneth   Dad.

Henry   He writes mostly.

Kenneth   What does he say?

Henry   What?

Kenneth   When he writes.

Henry   Him and Mum do a side each every other week.
They check I'm alright. Get worried you know.
He says how's things at work, I know what he
means, he means am I making money. I write
back and just say yeah Dad, yeah – everything

rosy. Everythings peachy as a picture, don't
you worry.

Kenneth Says that to me too. 'All well and good you going
on about Oxford, make sure you get yourself a
job.' Wants me to go into the civil service when I
graduate. I just laugh. That's as high as his
imagination can reach. That's the pinnacle of
ambition. Civil bloody service.

Henry Mum as well, every letter, how are things
Henry? Any girls take your fancy yet? She thinks
it's all tea parties and formal dancing. 'Take my
fancy.' Bloody hell. If she knew.

Kenneth Worried you're queer, probably.

Henry Watch it.

Kenneth

Henry Nah. She doesn't even know what that is.

Pause.

Kenneth What about this one tonight then?

Henry Hard to tell. Bit mouthy. Wait and see.

Kenneth How did you meet?

Henry I was putting up a poster on the billboard, and I
look down and there she is, staring up at me.
I'm like 'Hello love' . She says I've been
watching you. Big eyes. Says it you know –
suggestively. 'I've been *watching* you.' I went a bit
giddy if I'm honest. And she goes on, keeps on
talking telling me about herself, turns out she
works in this boutique, she's been watching all
morning. She says she liked my shoes. I said
they stop me falling off the ladder. We have a
drink at the end of the day, met up a few times
since then, you know, drink, pictures, the

preamble, and eventually last time I say why don't you come round mine, we'll have dinner.

Kenneth   You haven't got anything in.

Henry   I know, I'm aware of that. I wasn't thinking of the practicalities at that moment was I? But as a matter of fact she was, she says, 'You any good at cooking then?' I said 'As you mention it I don't know one end of a kitchen from the other but I'll have a go, I'll cook whatever you want, if you'll come over.' She liked that, and said it was alright, she'd bring the food and cook, if I got the drink.

Kenneth   Perfect lady.

Henry   Exactly.

Kenneth   Looks better doesn't it?

Henry   Suppose it does yeah.

    Beat.

Kenneth   A civil servant. Bloody hell. He doesn't have a clue.

Henry   What then?

Kenneth   A writer.

Henry   What sort?

Kenneth   A travel writer. I'm going to have a flat on the King's Road, full of ornaments, and carpets, collected from different countries and beautiful women, actresses, designers they'll all come over to visit.

Henry   Believe it when I see it Kenneth.

Kenneth   At Oxford they talk like this all the time, saying what they're going to do and how they're going to go about it, they tell you, I'm going to be a doctor, prime minister, I'm an *artist,* all these clever bastards, when they say things like that, it doesn't sound stupid at all because you know, you look at them and you think yes, yes, they probably will be what they want to be.

Henry   Rich most of them.

Kenneth   You've just got to want it enough.

The doorbell goes.

Henry   Right then.

Kenneth   What?

Henry   Off you go.

Kenneth   What?

Henry   In there.

Kenneth   Hang on.

Henry   That's what you said.

Kenneth   I can't not *meet* her.

Henry   I think you can.

Kenneth   It'll be rude if I don't even say hello.

Henry   No.

Kenneth   I'll meet her and then bugger off. Promise. Say I've got all this work to do.

Henry   . . .

Kenneth   . . .

Henry   You better put something on then.

Kenneth   I'm sure she won't mind.

Henry   She might not but I do. Scrawny little ferret running round the place.

The doorbell goes again.

At least do it up.

Kenneth *does.*

Henry *goes.*

Kenneth *undoes the dressing gown and checks himself in the mirror.*

Comes back and lights a cigarette.

Pours himself a drink. Looks relaxed.

Henry *enters with* **Sandra**.

Kenneth	Hello.
Sandra	Hello.
Henry	This is my brother Kenneth.
Kenneth	Ken.
Sandra	Hi Ken.
Henry	This is Sandra.
Sandra	How old are you?
Kenneth	What?
Sandra	How old are you? What's your age?
Kenneth	Nineteen. How old are you?
Sandra	Nineteen.
Kenneth	Coincidence.

Beat.

Sandra   Can I have one of those?

Kenneth   Course you can.

He gives her a cigarette.

Henry   Take your coat?

Sandra   Thank you.

Henry *takes her coat.* **Kenneth** *lights her cigarette.*

Sandra   Why aren't you dressed?

Kenneth	Don't need to be.
Sandra	You've been like that all day?
Kenneth	Yeah.
Sandra	Interesting.
Henry	He's a layabout.
Sandra	I like this.
Kenneth	Do you?
Sandra	Yes. It's very decadent. I like things that are decadent. Don't I Henry?
Henry	Yeah right.
Sandra	Henry's decadent.
Kenneth	Is he?
Sandra	He wears a leather jacket like Joe Orton. It's splendid. You must be a very decadent family.
Henry	Who's Joe Orton?
Sandra	Or maybe not.
Kenneth	He's a writer.
Sandra	Correct.
Kenneth	Our family's quite boring as it goes.
Sandra	All families are boring. That's why London was invented. So you can move away.
Kenneth	Yeah.
Sandra	Unless you're born in London. Then you're really in trouble.
Kenneth	Where are you from?
Sandra	Saffron Walden.
Kenneth	Where's that?

Sandra	It's a tiny little village in Essex, relatively pretty I suppose but the people are animals. Inbred most of them I think, couldn't wait to get out.
Kenneth	I know what you mean.
Sandra	Do you?
Kenneth	I like your dress.
Sandra	Do you live here?
Kenneth	I'm staying for a while.
Sandra	I see how lovely but normally, normally Kenneth, where are you based normally?
Kenneth	Based?
Sandra	Your *abode*.
Kenneth	I'm a student.
Sandra	Henry you're very quiet. A student?
Kenneth	Yes.
Sandra	Charming. Where?
Kenneth	Oxford.
Sandra	How silly.
Kenneth	What?
Sandra	Well I'm at Oxford too.
Kenneth	Henry didn't say.
Sandra	Henry probably doesn't know, do you? Henry?
Henry	
Sandra	Did you know I was at Oxford University?

Beat.

Henry	No.
Sandra	You see? We don't know each other that well at all really. I only met him a few weeks ago.

Henry	Two months now.
Sandra	Is it?
Henry	Yes.
Sandra	Well we've been having such fun, I must've lost track. When we met, I was working in my summer job. He was up a ladder doing his thing with the posters. I was working in a shop on Baker Street, Apples and Oranges, do you know it?
Kenneth	No.
Sandra	Delightful clothes. Wonderful colours. I simply adored it, but it's . . . well . . . it's turned into a complete disaster. Last week I got the sack.
Kenneth	Did you?
Sandra	I've never had the sack before, well I've never even had a job before and I was outraged. All of a sudden they told me to leave.
Kenneth	Why?
Sandra	I was smoking pot.
Kenneth	None of their business.
Sandra	While serving a customer.
Kenneth	Cool.
Sandra	That's what I thought, I thought that's in the spirit of the place, it's groovy, very now, they'll like it, but the customer complained didn't he, bloody bastard and they kicked me out on the street straight away. Don't know how I'm going to stay in London now with no job. Maybe I'll come here and live here with Henry. Would you like that Henry? Perhaps you'll still be hanging around Ken.
Henry	Kenneth do you need to –

Kenneth   What?

Henry   . . .

Kenneth   Oh. Right.

Henry   How about a drink?

Sandra   Whisky and ginger please.

Henry   Alright then.

Sandra   Kenneth are you having a drink?

Kenneth   No I . . . I'm going to go into my room actually. I've got some reading to get through. Great stack of books. I'll leave you and Henry to it.

Sandra   Reading?

Kenneth   Yes.

Sandra   You're joking?

Kenneth   Sorry.

Sandra   Well that's a shame. A real shame, Kenneth.

Kenneth   Busy.

Sandra   Why not stay for a little bit before you go all boring like that? Before you closet yourself away. Come on. Let's get to know each other.

Kenneth *considers.*

Kenneth   You don't mind, Henry, do you?

Henry *looks at* **Kenneth**.

Sandra   Kenneth, one drink?

Kenneth   Alright.

Sandra   Lovely.

Henry *gives her the drink and sits down, annoyed.*

Sandra *and* **Kenneth** *then sit together on the sofa.*

Sandra	I've got a confession to make actually. Can I tell you? I've been naughty.
Kenneth	Have you?
Sandra	You're from Oxford I expect you'll understand.
Kenneth	Go on.
Sandra	I'm completely gone.
Kenneth	Gone?
Sandra	Stoned.
Kenneth	Oh.
Sandra	Right this moment.
Kenneth	Yes.
Sandra	Not drunk.
Kenneth	No.
Sandra	Pot.
Kenneth	Good.
Sandra	I smoke too much of it I think.
Kenneth	I don't think that's possible.
Sandra	It's jolly isn't it?
Kenneth	I like it yes. Yes it is jolly.
Henry	
Sandra	I smoked my last before I came out, now it's all gone.
	And now we're all here and what are we going to do? Do you have any?
Henry	Did you bring dinner?
Sandra	What?
Henry	You were going to bring dinner, you were going to bring the ingredients and cook.

Sandra	It's your house.
Henry	We agreed.
Sandra	Well I'm sorry but I just assumed you would cook.
Henry	That's not what we said.
Sandra	
Henry	So we don't have anything in?
Sandra	Do you have any weed?
Henry	No.
Sandra	Then no we really don't have *anything* in then, Henry, not a thing. Very well done on this evening, nothing to eat nothing to smoke, what a wonderful party.
Henry	
Sandra	Maybe you should get some fish and chips.
Kenneth	I've got some.
Sandra	Fish and chips? Lovely.
Kenneth	Some weed.
Sandra	Even better.
Kenneth	In my room.
Sandra	Glorious.
Henry	You didn't tell me.
Kenneth	You don't like it.
Henry	You should've told me.
Kenneth	Why?
Sandra	Don't you go in for grass Henry?
Henry	
Sandra	?

Henry   Not legal is it?

Sandra   Henry! You're so amusing. Isn't he? Not legal.
                 The little policemen have got more important
                 things to think about these days, than this, no
                 one minds a bit of grass these days, it's like tea,
                 it's like water, it's like fresh air these days, no one
                 minds it at all. Go on Kenneth. Why don't you
                 get yourself up and go and fetch it?

Kenneth   Right you are.

                 He gets up and goes next door.

                 A moment.

                 Sandra *looks at* **Henry**.

Sandra   I don't like your hair.

Henry   It's always like this.

Sandra   I know.

                 Another moment.

                 Kenneth *comes back, sits down next to* **Sandra** *and starts
                 to roll.*

                 Pause.

Henry   You didn't tell me you'd lost your job.

Sandra   No.

Henry   Why not?

Sandra   We're not married Henry.

Henry   Didn't say we were but –

Sandra   Not even close. Don't want to get married.
                 Probably never will. There's no loyalty to you
                 Henry, I never promised anything.

Henry   So you say.

Sandra   So I do say that's right I say, I propose quite the
                 opposite of marriage, I think you're very

attractive and very nice, and all that but I don't
feel the need to make any kind of commitment,
especially one that restricts the woman in the
arrangement. I'm not ready to obey anyone. I
mean really, I'm not twenty yet, neither's
Kenneth, how old are you?

Henry   Twenty-three.

Sandra   Yes, well that's a bit older but we're not
our parents. Things are different now.
There's freedom.

Kenneth   Something's changing.

Sandra   Something's changing yes, that's right, that's
right Kenneth. You can feel it Henry, if you want
to. Even you. You're part of it, even you, you
moved to London, got your own place, did your
own things. You didn't stay at home in the same
town with your mum and dad, you're here and
you're really living, aren't you? It's marvellous.
What's the matter your face looks flat.

Henry   What?

Sandra   Don't you think?

Henry   What do you mean flat?

Sandra   All drooping, flat as a pancake, what's
the matter?

Beat.

Henry   I'm over here on my own.

Sandra   Oh.

So you are.

I'm sorry.

*She goes across and sits on the arm of his chair and hugs
him. Kisses his head.*

Have you been getting jealous?

You think I prefer your little brother, well he's nice I suppose but he's not a man is he? Not like you. He's a little boy.

Henry   He's got to read his books. Got to go to his room.

Kenneth   What?

Henry   Haven't you?

Kenneth   . . .

Henry

Kenneth   . . . Yeah.

Sandra   Henry?

You want him to stay in there all night.

Henry   Got his books.

Sandra   He can't stay in there all night.

Is he being simply gorgeous and getting out the way for us? Because I'm sorry but no, we can't do that. He's your guest, we can't evict him, turf him out, keep him all locked up in there, we can't do that.

Henry   Thought we'd want the place to ourselves.

Sandra   What if he needs the toilet?

Kenneth   He said I should use a bucket.

Sandra   Henry.

Henry   Thought you'd want some privacy Sandra.

Thought that's what you'd be after.

Up to you though.

Do what you like.

Sandra   We could have a little party instead.

Couldn't we? The three of us. Two brothers. You two, and me.

Yes. We should have a party.

What do you think?

Kenneth   Alright.

He lights the joint, and gets it going. Then gives it to **Sandra**.

She smokes it.

Sandra   I was out in the park all last night, with a group, a whole group of us, I think, the others I don't know what they did, but I drank wine until the early morning and then crawled under a tree and went to sleep. I slept until ten o'clock this morning. I was found by a policeman, by a little piggy, he said it's dangerous sweetheart you could've been raped, all by yourself in the park. I said the thing is *cunt*stable, the thing is you early morning irritating *cunt* . . . stable, I'm a woman, we could always be raped. At any moment, any minute of the day or night. If we lived our lives like that, trying to avoid it all the time, we wouldn't do anything. I looked at him, right in the face – I think he liked me – and I said, it's all about risk.

And then I turned and walked away. Went and had lunch, a joint, a bath and came here, but you know the thing – you two brothers – the thing was, I slept really well, just there, on the grass under the tree, I slept really well. I'm not sure about beds. I think we should sleep outside. I really think we should. Do you want some of this?

Henry   No.

She gives the spliff back to **Kenneth**. *He smokes it.*

Sandra   Do you like music?

Kenneth   Yes.

Sandra   Henry doesn't.

Henry   I do.

Sandra   Classical music.

Henry   Nothing wrong with that.

Sandra   Not rock and roll.

Henry   Well –

Sandra   Do you like rock and roll Kenneth?

Kenneth   I do yeah.

Sandra   What's your favourite rock and roll band?

Henry   He likes the Beatles.

Sandra   Is that right Kenneth? Do you like the Beatles?

Kenneth   Cream.

Sandra   You like Cream?

Kenneth   Yes.

Sandra   I like Cream.

Kenneth   Good.

Sandra   Henry? Do you like Cream?

Henry   . . .

Sandra   I don't mean the thing from cows.

Henry   Look, I'm rather tired of –

Sandra   What's your favourite song of theirs?

Henry   I don't know them very well that's true, I do
prefer classical music, yes, but that's allowed.

Sandra   It's allowed of course it is, but I think rock
and roll is better, don't you? Kenneth, don't
you think rock and roll is simply a better sort
of music?

Kenneth   Yeah I do.

Sandra   Do you know why Henry? Do you know why I
prefer it?

Henry   No.

Sandra   You can dance to it. I want to dance. Do you
have any music we can dance to? I love dancing.
It's form and chaos all at the same time.
Freedom and restriction combined. Anarchy
and fascism. I love it. Do you have any rock and
roll at all? You probably only have Mozart,
Beethoven . . . Tchaikovsky. You don't have
anything new. Do you?

Henry   No.

Sandra   That's a shame I felt like dancing. I really felt
like it tonight.

Henry

Kenneth   I've got some.

Sandra   Oh look, Kenneth has some records as well. He's
coming up with everything tonight isn't he?

Kenneth   Shall I get them?

Sandra   Why not?

     Kenneth *goes.*

   Beat.

Sandra   Are you going to dance Henry?

Henry   No.

Sandra   Well why don't you go to the fish and chip shop
then, because I'm getting hungry and you don't

have any food I remember now because of the mix up, so why don't you be a darling and go to the fish and chip shop and get us all fish and chips and while you're away, me and Kenneth, we'll have a bit of a dance.

Henry   A dance.

Sandra   Yes.

You know what dancing is.

Henry *is angry. Stands up, gets his coat.*

Kenneth *comes back in holding a small pile of records.*

Kenneth   Where are you going?

Henry   Fish and chips.

Kenneth   Oh right. Good. You . . . Are you . . .?

Henry   Back in ten minutes.

He goes.

Sandra   Never seen him so red in the face.

Kenneth   He gets angry sometimes.

Sandra   He takes it all so seriously.

Kenneth   Nothing to worry about.

Sandra   He's old fashioned.

Kenneth   He likes you.

Beat.

Sandra   Are you old fashioned Kenneth?

Kenneth   No.

I get bored easily. I like new things.

I like things that are fresh.

Sandra   Fresh.

Kenneth *looks through the records.*

Sandra	The world's going to be a different place in ten years, everything's that's stopping us, what we're told to do, what we're told is the way to live, it'll all be different, you can feel it.
Kenneth	Yeah.
Sandra	It's us, it's people like you and me Kenneth.
Kenneth	I know.
Sandra	Young people, our age. We're the moment. Henry's just that bit too old he can't understand.
Kenneth	He's always been old.
Sandra	I love being like this, I can feel the muscles in my body, I look in the mirror, there's not a wrinkle on my face, I wake up more vital.
Kenneth	Fresh.
Sandra	Fresh yes. We don't need ties, we don't need jobs. We don't need these *structures*.
Kenneth	Yeah.
Sandra	Or clothes. Looking like this, like we do, like you do under that look at you. You could walk around wearing nothing and you'd look better than most people when they're dressed up, you know that?
Kenneth	Well you too.
Sandra	
Kenneth	I don't want to be rude but I imagine you look quite lovely under that.

They look at each other.

Sandra	My older sister, she's only five years older than me but she's falling apart. I know I'm not the most beautiful girl in the world, and it's not about looks it's about feeling, the feeling of now,

	I want to stay this age, in this summer, doing what I'm doing, for the rest of my life.
Kenneth	You could be a model or something.
Sandra	A model.
Kenneth	Yeah.
Sandra	A model what?
Kenneth	In a magazine. Advertising holidays or perfume or something.
Sandra	A model woman you mean.
Kenneth	Yeah.
Sandra	I wonder what you think that is?
Kenneth	What?
Sandra	A model woman.
Kenneth	He said you were a feminist.
Sandra	You and him ever shared?
Kenneth	Shared?
Sandra	A woman.
Kenneth	No.
Sandra	I don't mean shared.
Kenneth	I know what you mean.
Sandra	I mean kissed.
Kenneth	Kissed.
Sandra	Have you ever kissed the same woman.
Kenneth	No.
Sandra	I like you Kenneth.
Kenneth	I know, I know that I can tell but he'll be back.
Sandra	What do you mean?

Beat.

Kenneth   He's my brother.

Sandra   I know he is.

But.

Well.

Here's what would happen. He'd be upset, in the moment, he'd be angry and leave, walk out the door, go to the pub, he'd call you a bastard want you to leave, to move out, but in a day or two, maybe even in a few hours, he'd get over it, think of it as a good thing that happened, because we're nothing me and him we're just passing through, he knows that really.

You're running your hand through your hair, I think you do that when you get nervous, when someone's putting you under pressure, but there's no pressure Kenneth. You can do what you like.

I like you.

And let's be clear, Kenneth.

You haven't stopped looking at me since I came through the door have you?

Kenneth   No.

Sandra   Not since I came through the door.

Kenneth   No.

Sandra   So we could just dance a little couldn't we? At least. Until he gets back.

Kenneth   . . .

Sandra   We're going to die.

Kenneth   What?

Sandra   We're going, to die.

Kenneth   Not now.

Sandra   Eventually, and the world is terrible, with Russia,

and the bomb

and Vietnam,

and all we're asking for, people like you and me,
all we're asking for, is some humanity, is some
freedom, is to throw off everything that holds us
down and explore what we could do instead.
Maybe it doesn't have to be about power and
guns and money, maybe it could just be about
the fact that underneath, underneath our
background and our countries and our clothes,
like we said, we're all the same. That's all that
people like you and me, that's all we're saying.
We're going to die, and we shouldn't waste our
lives. Don't you agree Kenneth?

Kenneth   Yes I do.

Sandra   The summer's only just started.

We could go off together, see what happens.

What do you think?

We could have adventures together you and me.

Kenneth   Adventures?

Sandra   You chosen something to dance to then?

Kenneth looks at the records and smokes, then suddenly
remembers, he smiles, looks at his watch, gives the joint to
Sandra*, runs, jumps over the sofa again, and switches on*
the television.

We hear the opening of 'All You Need Is Love'.

Sandra   What's this?

Kenneth   The Beatles.

Sandra   It doesn't seem like music you can dance to.

Kenneth   I can dance to anything.

He takes her hand and they dance close and smoke as the Beatles play.

They kiss.

He holds her hand and they look at each other.

Henry *comes in the door.*

Henry   They're shut.

He sees them.

Kenneth *backs off.*

Henry *looks at them.*

Sandra   Henry. It's alright. It doesn't matter.

It's alright.

She goes towards him.

Touches him.

What's the problem?

She touches his face.

He looks at her.

He turns to **Kenneth**.

Kenneth   I'm . . . we just . . .

Sorry.

Henry *goes back out the door and shuts it behind him.*

Kenneth'*s upset, goes and turns down the television.*

Kneels by it.

Sandra   Tomorrow he'll come back and you'll sort it all out. You'll explain how it happened. That we're better suited, that it's not a one night thing, that we're going to live together in Oxford next term.

Kenneth   We –

Sandra   We could do that, couldn't we? And you'll tell him that we're going to travel around together this summer, and he'll listen and understand and within a month he'll look back on this moment as being one of the best things that's happened to him, especially when he's found a new girl to go out with, one that's really suited to him, a slightly duller traditional kind of girl. When he finds her, at that point, he'll be really pleased this happened.

Sometimes you have to do what feels right.

Kenneth   Yeah I know.

Sandra   One day we'll laugh about this.

Kenneth   Yes.

I mean . . .

I don't think he even liked you that much.

Sandra   Oh.

Kenneth   I think you're lovely. All of you.

They move closer.

Sandra   The whole of the summer, we can do whatever we want.

So.

Are you ready?

Kenneth   For?

Sandra   Adventures.

Lights fade.

Curtain.

End of Act One.

Two

She Bangs the Drums by the Stone Roses

Evening. March 1990. The dining/living room of a medium-sized terraced house on the outskirts of Reading. Reasonably tidy. A large table in the middle. Family photos. A television is muted, but showing scenes of the television news, riots in London.

The music is playing out of a stereo on the side.

Jamie, *14, enters, performing and singing. Really enjoying himself. He jumps on the table, sings and dances to a surprising amount of the song. He knows all the words and intonation – he's talented.*

Suddenly there's a noise from off, a key in the door, as it opens.

From off:

Kenneth   Jamie?!

           Jamie *is surprised, nearly falls off the table, knocks over some flowers, crashes into a bookshelf.*

Kenneth   See it's still in one piece,

Sandra   Alright

Kenneth   Hasn't exploded, blown over, burnt down, he hasn't taken it apart piece by piece it's exactly as you left it.

           Jamie *tries to tidy up as* **Kenneth** *enters. He's now 42, wearing a jacket, shirt and trousers. He still looks youngish. He takes his coat off.*

Kenneth   What are you up to?

Jamie   Nothing.

Kenneth   What's this?

Jamie   The Stone Roses

           Kenneth *listens for a second.*

Kenneth   He can't sing.

Jamie   Neither can you Dad.

Kenneth   Watch it.

Jamie   Doesn't stop you trying.

Kenneth   The ungrateful child.

Jamie   No.

Kenneth   I give you all this. And you spit in my face.

Jamie   I don't understand.

Kenneth   Switch it off.

He dumps his coat and goes out again.

Jamie *stops the tape. Ejects it.*

From off:

Kenneth   She could've been stuck there playing to no one, tears rolling down her face.

Rose   It's alright.

Kenneth   She was trying to hide it but I could see, she was upset.

Jamie *puts the tape carefully back in the box.*

Sits on the arm of the sofa and listens.

Kenneth *comes back in. He's followed by* **Rose***, 16, in school uniform, with her violin.*

Kenneth (*about the television*)   Turn that off too.

Jamie   There's a riot going on.

Kenneth   Not tonight / there isn't,

Rose   Dad –

Kenneth   She was upset!

Jamie   It's in London, there's horses and skinheads.

Rose	It doesn't matter.
Jamie	Do you pay poll tax / Dad?
Kenneth	It's one day a year Sandra you know what I'm saying, she had a concert and it's nearly her birthday and it meant something to her.

Rose *goes and sits in a chair.*

Kenneth *looks round.* **Sandra***'s not there.*

Kenneth	Where is she?
Rose	Kitchen.
Kenneth	Thought she was following.
Rose	She said she had something to prepare.
Kenneth	Oh.

He sits down.

Jamie you should've come, she was brilliant, like Jacqueline du Pré.

Jamie	Jacqueline du Pré's / a cellist.
Kenneth	Solo and everything, little bit / she had to get right.
Rose	You know what he meant. (*To* **Kenneth**.) It wasn't / a solo.
Kenneth	Everyone looking, everyone's asking, who's that girl with the cello?
Rose	/ Violin
Kenneth	She's amazing.
Jamie	Don't like classical / music.
Kenneth	I was right there sweetheart, front row.
Rose	Yeah.
Kenneth	Saved a seat for your mother, that was a waste of time.

Jamie	Can I go upstairs?
Kenneth	No. We're doing a cake.
Jamie	Why?
Rosie	A cake.
Kenneth	Yes.
Rosie	Mum said you were doing a surprise.
Kenneth	Oh.
	Well.
	It's a cake.
Jamie	Why?
Kenneth	It's nearly your sister's birthday.
Jamie	When?
Kenneth	Midnight.
Jamie	How old is she?
Kenneth	Come on Jamie.
Jamie	I don't know. How old?
Kenneth	. . .
Jamie	Dad
Kenneth	Fifteen
Rose	Sixteen.
Kenneth	I thought you were fifteen.
Rose	Doesn't matter.

Beat.

Kenneth	What about your friends love? Were they there?
Rose	It's a weeknight.
Kenneth	You getting on with them alright now?
Rose	Dad . . .

Kenneth	What?
Rose	Can we not talk about this please?
Kenneth	Why not?
Rose	It's private?
Kenneth	It's only your brother.
Jamie	I won't tell anyone. What happened?
Rose	/ Shut up.
Kenneth	Your music teacher, what's his name?
Rose	Mr / Parsons.
Kenneth	You know he went to Oxford?
Rose	Thought I saw you talking.
Kenneth	He must've been there the same time as your mother and me, an organ scholar apparently, don't remember him but organ scholars were strange.
Rose	He is / strange.
Kenneth	We didn't really move in the same / circles.
Rose	He smarms up to the parents, but in the classroom he's a total Hitler.
Kenneth	One of those?
Rose	Yeah.
Jamie	He's alright with me.
Rose	Right.
Jamie	Yeah. I like him.
Rosie	Do you.
Jamie	It's probably cos you're stupid he only likes clever people.

Rosie   I really hate you.

Beat.

Kenneth   Well if he gives you trouble, love, you let
me know.

Rose   What? Are you going to beat him up?

Kenneth   No I'll get him on the phone and have a word.
The power of rhetoric, much forgotten.

Rose   I can't imagine you hitting anyone Dad.

Kenneth   Definitely / not.

Rose   But isn't that what Dads are supposed to do?

Kenneth   What?

Rose   Look after their daughters.

Jamie   I can hit people. / I've got a really good punch.

Kenneth   Rosie don't be stupid you're looked after you get
everything you want.

Rose   / No.

Kenneth   Where is she? Thought we were having cake.

He gets up and goes out.

Rose (*to herself*)   He never *listens* . . .

Jamie   I hit someone last week.

Rose   Shut up.

Jamie   After maths club we were giving each other
dead arms.

Rose   / 'Maths club'.

Jamie   Paul nearly cried when I got him.

Rose   Can't believe you go to maths club.

Jamie   What?

Rose	Such a geek.
Jamie	I'll hit you.
Rose	You're too old to hit girls.
Jamie	It's different with sisters.
Rose	No it isn't. I'm a woman now. I can say what I want, and you can't do anything.

He looks at her.

Jamie   Daniel's brother said that last Saturday at some party he burst into a bedroom and found Sarah Franks doing something to Mark Edwards that involved his penis.

Rose

Jamie   Isn't Mark Edwards supposed to be your boyfriend?

Rose   . . .

Jamie   Thought so.

You see? Don't need to hit you.

Happy birthday.

Cake makes you fat.

He goes out.

Rose *sits there. Upset. Doesn't know what to do.*

A moment.

Kenneth *comes back in.*

Kenneth   Wish I'd learnt an instrument. But we didn't have the facilities you do these days, and anyway, we all wanted to play guitar or drums, you've seen the photo. Classical took a back seat. You've seen the photo?

Rose   Yeah.

Kenneth	Where's your brother gone?
Rose	Said he didn't want any cake.
Kenneth	Not the point.
Rose	Doesn't matter.
Kenneth	Jamie come down here!
Rose	Dad –
Kenneth	If you're not down in two minutes I'm sending your mother! That'll work.

He winks at **Rose**.

Kenneth	Your uncle likes classical. We should invite him one day to see you. But anyway it's all the same thing now though isn't it? McCartney used to say it, these *divisions* between genres well they're pointless, I mean actually what's the difference between Mozart and Procol Harum, essentially they're the same thing.
Rose	What's Procol Harum?
Kenneth	What?
Rose	What's Procol Harum?
Kenneth	Who not what.
Rose	They're a band then?
Kenneth	*What's Procol Harum?*
Rose	Okay it doesn't / matter.
Kenneth	This weekend, we're getting the records out Rosie.
Rose	Dad – really –
Kenneth	You and me.
Rose	No.
Kenneth	Yes. If you haven't heard of Procol Harum you haven't lived.

Rose	Just tell me
Kenneth	Impossible.
Rose	Dad.
Kenneth	No. You have to hear them. In for a treat.
Rose	. . .
Kenneth	Jamie! Now! We'll listen to it this weekend. Something to look forward to.
Rose	I think there is a difference.
Kenneth	What?
Rose	I think there is a difference between –

Sandra *enters with a bottle of wine and a glass.*

Sandra	I am completely dry. My throat is like Ethiopia or somewhere. Absolutely desperate for a glass or two. What's the matter love you look like you've been hit by a car.
Kenneth	Rose was talking love.
Sandra	Were you? Go on then. Wasn't interrupting. Go on. Speak.
Rose	I was just / saying about –
Kenneth	Did you get me one of those?
Sandra	One of these?
Kenneth	Yes.
Sandra	A *glass* you mean Kenneth?
Kenneth	A glass yes.
Sandra	You want a glass.
Kenneth	Unless you expect me to drink it from the bottle?
Sandra	I wouldn't mind.

Kenneth	I'm sure you wouldn't but some of us have standards.
Sandra	You know where the kitchen is.

He gets up.

Kenneth	You want one Rose?
Sandra	Brilliant parenting Kenneth.
Kenneth	Celebration isn't it?
Rose	I'm fine.
Sandra	Perhaps she wants a fag too.
Rose	No thanks.
Sandra	Sarcasm love.
Kenneth	She's fifteen.
Rose	Sixteen.
Kenneth	Sixteen there you are. We were drinking at that age, we drank for England both of us / you've told me the things you did.
Sandra	Not with my parents, we drank secretly, and I bet she does that a lot, sure she's got places she goes –
Rose	No / actually
Sandra	She doesn't want to drink with us, we're *boring*.
Kenneth	We are boring, that's true.
Sandra	We're like dinosaurs to her.
Kenneth	Jamie! Last chance!
Sandra	You're like a mammoth Ken, and I'm . . . I'm one of those things.
Kenneth	What things?
Sandra	One of those flying things.

She mimes, and makes the noise.

Kenneth   Are you sure you don't want a glass love?

Rose   Yeah.

Sandra   What are they called?

She mimes and does the noise again.

Kenneth   Shall I bring the cake in?

Sandra   Ken! No. Let's wait till midnight. / What's –

Rose   I'm tired.

Sandra   It'll be fun. You can stay up. See it in. You're only sixteen once.

Rose   Yeah but . . .

Kenneth   Alright.

He goes.

A moment.

Sandra   What are they called those flying dinosaurs?

Rosie   Pterodactyls.

Sandra   Terro-dactles. That's it! My daughter is a genius, she thinks and plays the violin, look at you. All dressed up.

Rosie   It's uniform.

Sandra   Oh sweetheart, you're sulking, why are you sulking?

Rose   I'm not.

Sandra   Long face.

Rose   Just because I'm not getting drunk doesn't / mean I'm unhappy.

Sandra   I'm not drunk darling, I am / seriously not drunk.

Rose	But you keep on / interrupting and that is getting quite annoying.
Sandra	I am tired. I'll give you that, I am extremely exhausted from a long day . . . what?
Rose	Nothing.

Beat.

Sandra	You have to learn, that sometimes, sometimes in life, people are late.
Rose	I *know*. I've told you it doesn't matter. I'm / not bothered.
Sandra	But obviously it does, it's this huge rift between us tonight I mean I'd give you a hug but I'm not allowed to touch you anymore now that you're a teenager. I know I know that you are not happy I can see it. I am *concerned*. But your father and me we work hard and sometimes these things can't be avoided.
	You're not a kid anymore are you?
	You can understand what I'm saying.
	Yes?
Rose	. . .
Sandra	Are you seeing Mark / this weekend?
Rose	It was just before, when all the other parents were all there. Before it began.
Sandra	Oh – no. We're still / on this.
Rose	It was embarrassing. All the other parents were there. Dad only got there at the last minute, and you –
Sandra	I'm very busy Rose.
Rose	You're a modern mother a working woman / I know I know

Sandra	These other mums are probably at home all day, probably don't work the hours I do.
Rose	I think they do actually. Most of them do work.
Sandra	I drove foot to floor, top speed, all the way there, broke the law for you.
Rose	Thanks that's really / nice of you.
Sandra	And I got there for your bit. Didn't I?
Rose	
Sandra	Didn't I?
	Rosie?
	Did you see me?
Rose	No.
Sandra	I was at the back, standing at the back.
Rose	Didn't see you Mum.

Sandra *looks at her.*

Sandra	What's the matter with you tonight? Your father's right, have a glass.

Sandra *offers her the glass.*

Rose	No.
Sandra	Come on love you need it. Long face like that.
Rose	What about you?
Sandra	Don't worry about me, I am of a generation where we improvise wildly.

Rose *takes the glass.* **Sandra** *swigs from the bottle as* **Kenneth** *enters with a glass.*

Kenneth	That's the woman I fell in love with right there. / Look at that.
Sandra	You should keep it going.
Rose	What?

Sandra	The violin. What grade are you now?
Rose	You don't know?
Sandra	No I don't know that's why I'm / asking.
Rose	We went out?
Kenneth	She's grade seven.
Rose	*Six*.
Kenneth	Thought it was / seven.
Rose	I passed last month. Remember?
Kenneth	I thought –
Rose	We went out for dinner.
Kenneth	Oh right yes. You . . .
Rose	I got a distinction we went out / to celebrate.
Kenneth	Thought that was seven.
Rose	No.
Sandra	Grade six that's really something. You could keep it going Rosie – a professional musician. Touring the world.
Rose	Pays really bad –
Sandra	It's not about the money, it's the passion, the audiences. You enjoy playing don't you? I can tell.
Rose	Can we just have the cake now?
Sandra	The look on your face when you get it right. Concentration. A little smile. I saw you. It's important to do something you love.
Rose	Yeah. Can we do the cake / though?
Kenneth	We'll wait for midnight, it's what your mother / wants.

Sandra   It's not all about money.

Kenneth   Do you remember that little orchestra at the Isle of Wight?

Sandra   I do.

Kenneth   With a hangover it was / marvellous.

Sandra   I remember the journey home.

Rose   Can I / go upstairs then please?

Sandra   Trying to hitch. Hungover, tired, smelling of crap, your father was irresponsible at that age love, please don't ever copy his behaviour. We nearly ended up murdered – this truck driver looking at my legs, your father encouraging him.

Kenneth   We didn't have any money.

Rose   I've heard this story so many times.

Kenneth   He needed paying. That was the deal.

Sandra   You were my pimp.

Kenneth   It was different, you could do things / like that then.

Sandra   I suppose I did have very good legs.

Kenneth   All art aspires to the quality of music sweetheart, you know who said that?

Rose   / Yes.

Sandra   You could do it at university.

Kenneth   T.S. Elliot.

Rose   / Walter Pater

Sandra   A degree in music, you can do that at Oxford can't you?

Kenneth   You can, we were saying, like your Mr –

Sandra	What?
Kenneth	Her music teacher I was speaking to Mr –
Sandra	What are you talking about?
Kenneth	He was an organ scholar at Oxford, Mr –
Rose	Parsons.
Kenneth	Parsons right.
Sandra	Are you doing music A level Rosie?
Rose	Oh. – fucking . . .
Sandra	Fucking. What fucking?
Rose	Just –
Sandra	Fucking, Ken, she's saying fucking.
Kenneth	Yes I know.
Sandra	Love, why are you swearing you must be upset.
Rose	We talked about my A levels *last week*!
Sandra	Don't get offended Rosie. I've got a life of my own. I can't remember every detail. What did we say then? What did we decide? You're doing music then, yes?
	Yes?
Rose	Yes.
Sandra	Good. Well then you can keep that going, get your degree then join an orchestra, tour the world, perfect, all sorted out, get Jamie down here I'm on a roll.
Kenneth	Jamie!
Rose	I'm going upstairs
Sandra	Sweetheart no, we have a cake.

Beat.

Rose   I'll come down for midnight, alright?

Sandra   You don't enjoy our company.

Rose   I'm going to make a phone call.

Sandra   It's half eleven, who are you calling at this time, it's too late, they'll be in bed.

Rose   We're not in bed.

Sandra   Who is it?

Rose   I don't have to tell you / who I'm calling.

Sandra   Have I offended you Rosie?

Kenneth   It's alright love, off you go, we'll call you when it's / time.

Sandra   Did I bring you up like this? This look, this contempt?

Kenneth   Leave her alone.

Sandra   Rejecting your parents it's an important part of growing up I understand that, teenage rebellion's important, but I have to say sweetheart tonight would not be the time, you don't seem grateful, your father and I we made a real effort.

Rose   You nearly missed the concert Mum. When you came in late, everyone *looked*.

Sandra

Rose

Sandra   I haven't told you this before but I'm not sure about Mark.

Kenneth   Sandra –

Sandra   He's a nice boy I know but –

Rose   What?

Kenneth	Sandra shut the mouth now / the mouth is doing things.
Sandra	He flirts with me, and I know he's a / teenager, the hormones but –
Rose	What are you talking about?
Sandra	He flirts with me in the kitchen.
Rose	No he doesn't.
Sandra	He does, when he's here, I mean I'm not bothered by it but you should probably know. It's understandable, boys like real women at that age, fully formed, you know, and there's plenty more fish for you, in the sea, that's all I'm saying. Don't get too attached.
Rose	Fuck's sake mum you're a bitch.
Kenneth	Can't argue with that love.
Sandra	I'm a *bitch*, I love this swearing, it's very sweet, isn't it Kenneth? She really is / growing up.
Kenneth	It's alright Rosie off you go, your mother's / showing off
Sandra	Oh look at you, all little and upset and red – you're young is what I'm saying, and you're pretty, when you make the effort. You look so miserable. You should be having fun.
Rose	Like you had fun you mean.
Sandra	Well yes it's true we did have *fun* when we were your age we did.
Rose	Fucked around a lot did you?
Sandra	We certainly weren't hung up on sex no.
Rose	Now you think I'm *hung up on sex*.

Sandra	We didn't put all our eggs in one basket, it all seems so important for you, and you've got all these exams, I'm worried, you look depressed.
Rose	Not my fault about the exams.
Sandra	No but –
Rose	So what are you saying?
Sandra	. . .
Rose	
Sandra	Fine. Don't listen to me. Do what you want. Make your mistakes and when you come running I'll be here to pick up the pieces, you've always got me darling, you'll always have me looking after you, that's what mothers do.
Kenneth	Off you go love.
Rose	Don't shout yeah, while I'm on the phone.
Sandra	Don't be silly.
Rose	Cos you do sometimes and it's embarrassing.

She goes.

Pause.

Sandra *goes to a cupboard, takes out her cigarettes.*

Kenneth *watches her.*

She lights a cigarette.

Kenneth	You look tired.
Sandra	Thanks.
Kenneth	That was a mess tonight.
Sandra	
Kenneth	It's not fair.

Sandra	I've done the same for you Kenneth. Filled in for you.
Kenneth	Not like this, I've never just forgotten entirely.
Sandra	It shouldn't have happened I know that.
Kenneth	Right, and when she called from the payphone asking where you were I –
Sandra	You shouldn't have left Jamie by himself.
Kenneth	He's fourteen.
Sandra	He's weird.
Kenneth	He's bright.
Sandra	That's the problem.
Kenneth	It was a couple of hours. I told him not to touch anything. I gave him a number to call if he needed to. I couldn't leave her there playing to no-one, it obviously means a lot to her. And he wouldn't come with me of course.
Sandra	. . .
Kenneth	He could've gone next door in an emergency.
Sandra	Next door.
Kenneth	Yes.
Sandra	Don't want next door looking after him.
Kenneth	What?
Sandra	Don't trust them.
Kenneth	Why not?
Sandra	
Kenneth	Why not?
Sandra	They're loud.

Kenneth   Loud.

Sandra   Always shouting.

Kenneth   Remind you of anyone?

Sandra   Not like we do, nothing like us, they do it in public, out the door, they seem a bit violent if you ask me.

Kenneth   Up to them how they want to be, none of our business.

Sandra   Up to them alright yes yes, although it's annoying first thing in the morning when you want some peace and quiet, sorting out your car first thing and there she is, the mum, shouting her face off out the front door.

Not sure how they're even in that house. They can't have bought it.

Not being . . .

You know what I mean.

It's not cheap round here.

Pause.

Kenneth   The bill came today.

Sandra   What?

Kenneth   School fees.

Sandra   How much?

Kenneth   . . .

Sandra   Christ.

Kenneth   I know.

So.

Beat.

What was it tonight?

Sandra	A meeting.
Kenneth	With?
Sandra	Chris.

Beat.

Kenneth	Chris again.
Sandra	What? Chris again yes again Chris again yes. What?
Kenneth	These late meetings.
Sandra	It's busy at the moment we don't get a chance in the days and then we bump into each other at five o'clock and we're like oh God there's about twelve things we need to sort out before tomorrow so we have to sit down and go through them there and then.
Kenneth	Sit down?
Sandra	Yes, we sit down.
Kenneth	What do you mean?
Sandra	A meeting.
Kenneth	You sit down.
Sandra	Yes we sit down we tried standing up but our legs got tired.
Kenneth	Where?
Sandra	What?
Kenneth	Where do you sit down together?
Sandra	Alright Columbo.
Kenneth	Just a question. Don't make me / feel stupid asking.
Sandra	'Sit down together.'
Kenneth	Sandra I'm not –

Sandra	You're implying something.
Kenneth	When you arrived tonight you smelt of gin.
Sandra	We had a drink together.
Kenneth	A drink together.
Sandra	Together yes.
Kenneth	Always *together*.
Sandra	It's kind of what a *meeting* implies, Kenneth.

Kenneth	So the meeting was . . .
Sandra	Yes? The meeting was . . . what?
Kenneth	Where. Where was the meeting?
Sandra	Well . . .

She looks at him.

Sometimes we go to the pub, shocking I know but it's the evening and we can't *bear* to stay in the office. Look at you. Your face quivering. Me and him in the pub. Ooo what might happen. Kenneth you think I'm having an affair.

Kenneth	How many?
Sandra	Affairs? None.
Kenneth	Not affairs. How many –
Sandra	Meetings? With Chris? We *work together*.
Kenneth	How many gins?
Sandra	Gins.
Kenneth	Before you drove.
Sandra	Oh how many gins. I see. I don't know.
Kenneth	That's the worst answer to that question.
Sandra	A couple?

Kenneth	A couple like two, or a couple like five.
Sandra	Like two.
Kenneth	*Like* two?
Sandra	Oh stop.
Kenneth	Stop what? You're all over the place I think you're completely off the leash at the moment, I don't know what you're up to.

A moment.

Sandra	Alright.
Kenneth	What?
Sandra	What if I was?
Kenneth	What?
Sandra	Having an affair, what if I was?
Kenneth	Are you?
Sandra	Let's have a conversation.
Kenneth	So you are.
Sandra	No. But what if I was?
Kenneth	I'm not playing a game. Not tonight. We can do this some other time.
Sandra	Ken . . .
Kenneth	What? This is hypothetical or something.
Sandra	Yes! Hypothetical. Exactly.
Kenneth	I'm serious. I want to talk to you, I want you to be honest, this isn't funny.
Sandra	I'm just talking Kenneth. I'm just asking what you'd do if I was.
Kenneth	This is a test now?
Sandra	This is a question.

Kenneth   You mean you want to.

Sandra   There's something up with you tonight.

Kenneth   I've had enough. Yes, / I've had enough –

Sandra   I want a conversation Kenneth. We've always been able to do that.

Kenneth   Alright.

Sandra   You wouldn't want to trap me.

Kenneth   So you feel trapped?

Sandra   Hypothetically.

Kenneth   Of course I don't want to trap you, / where does that –

Sandra   We always said we've always said there's nothing worse than being stuck.

Kenneth   So what have you done?

Sandra   Because we're going to die.

Kenneth   What have you done?

Sandra   Nothing.

     Beat.

Kenneth   We're going to die, that's true Sandra, a rare admission on your part, death approaches, so what have you –

Sandra   When I look in the mirror these days I see a ghost.

Kenneth   The cigarettes don't help.

Sandra   Decay. All the time.

Kenneth   So what are you saying?

     A moment.

Kenneth   You've found someone.

Sandra	This is going round and round your head isn't it?
Kenneth	Someone younger.
Sandra	Someone *younger*? No.
Kenneth	Or older. Chris.
Sandra	I haven't found anyone I'm asking a question. I'm simply inviting a discussion about a subject but you're getting all jumpy and twitchy about it – *Chris*?
Kenneth	You can tell me.
Sandra	*Chris*? No.
Kenneth	Really.
	Tell me honestly.
Sandra	Kenneth.
Kenneth	Honestly.
Sandra	Chris?
Kenneth	I'll go first.
Sandra	Go first at what?
Kenneth	I'll lay it out.
Sandra	Ken –
Kenneth	The truth. We haven't properly talked for –
Sandra	We're very busy.
Kenneth	I have.
Sandra	Have what?
Kenneth	I have slept with someone else.
Sandra	You . . .
	Beat.
Kenneth	Your turn.

Sandra   Wait wait.

Kenneth   Okay. I've said it. Your turn.

A moment. She looks at him.

Sandra   You. . .

Kenneth   I'm not the only one am I?

Sandra   I was talking hypothetically.

Kenneth   Come on

Sandra   What?

Kenneth   The meetings, the secrets.

Sandra   What secrets?

Kenneth   We can talk about the details when / it's out.

Sandra   No we can talk about the details now.

Kenneth   Who was it?

Sandra   There isn't / anyone.

Kenneth   Chris?

Sandra   No. Chris? No. Chris is ridiculous. For fuck's sake Kenneth.

Kenneth   Right.

I thought . . .

Sandra   No.

Kenneth   Right.

Shit.

Sandra   More wine?

She pours more wine.

Sandra   So?

Let's have it.

Kenneth   I was angry. I met a girl. Her name was Frankie.

Sandra   That's a boy's name.

Kenneth   And a girl's name I believe.

Sandra   Are you sure it wasn't a boy?

Kenneth   Yeah.

Sandra   How do you know?

Kenneth   I know.

She takes that in.

Sandra   How old?

Kenneth   Does it matter?

Sandra   I'm not angry here Kenneth.

Kenneth   Yes but –

Sandra   Look at me, look at my body language my expression.

Kenneth   Alright.

Sandra   You see I'm acting surprisingly calm considering I'm the victim.

Kenneth   You're never the victim.

Sandra   You've messed me around.

Kenneth   Yes.

Sandra   Yes so does it matter? It matters to me. So.

Kenneth   Alright.

Sandra   How old?

Kenneth   Look –

Sandra   HOW OLD?

Kenneth   Early twenties?

Sandra   What does she do?

Kenneth   I don't know.

Sandra   Did you catch a surname in the course of
the evening?

Kenneth

Sandra

Kenneth   Exactly. You're right. That's exactly what it was
like.

Sandra   In and out.

Kenneth   Bit more to it than that but –

Sandra   In essence.

Kenneth   Yeah

Sandra   BLOODY HELL KEN. BLOODY FUCKING
HELL.

Kenneth   I'm sorry.

Pause.

Sandra   FRANKIE.

Kenneth   Frankie.

She looks at him.

A moment.

Sandra   Cigarette?

Kenneth   Don't be stupid.

She rolls a cigarette across the table.

He looks at it.

She throws him the lighter.

A moment.

He lights up.

Sandra   Blonde?

Kenneth   No.

Sandra	Redhead?
Kenneth	Brunette.
Sandra	Tall?
Kenneth	Ish.
Sandra	Looked like me did she?
Kenneth	No she –
Sandra	From the little you remember?
Kenneth	From what I can remember she wasn't a patch on you.
Sandra	Oh.

Beat.

Kenneth	But yes, she was . . .
Sandra	She was . . . what? She was what?
Kenneth	Fresh.
Sandra	Fresh.
Kenneth	
Sandra	Fresh *meat*.
Kenneth	If you like.
Sandra	Right.
Kenneth	Yes.
Sandra	Yes.
Kenneth	Yes she smelt different.
Sandra	You're not sorry.
Kenneth	Not sorry.
Sandra	Are you? You love me, your feelings towards me are exactly the same but you had a great time with her you just had a really good new kind of sex.

Kenneth   Yeah.

Sandra   Then don't apologise then. If you're not sorry, take it back.

Kenneth   . . .

Sandra   TAKE IT BACK!

Kenneth   Alright.

> **Rose** *bursts in, crying.*

Rose   I told you both to shut up and you're shouting your bloody mouths off, I told you and Mark was on the phone and he was like what's that? And I tried to tell him it was the television but he thought you were shouting at me, he said it clearly wasn't a good time and hung up but we had to *talk* about something, it gave him an excuse to – now I have to go into school tomorrow and – Oh –

> *She sees* **Kenneth** *with a cigarette.*

Rose   What, you're smoking now?

Kenneth

Rose

Sandra

Rose   Fucking hell you two are the shittest fucking parents. I fucking hate you.

> *She storms out.*

Sandra   Five minutes sweetheart.

> **Rose** *has gone.*

Kenneth   You understand why I did it. I think you know.

Sandra   No I don't know.

Kenneth	That's why you're not angry, there was a bit of you that wanted this, you want me to do something exactly like this.
Sandra	I was happy with you.
Kenneth	No you wanted something more, that's why you started this hypothetical thing you wanted me to say –
Sandra	Kenneth I love you, I'm a lucky girl most men your age are sagging, but look at you –
Kenneth	You could go for someone younger then.
Sandra	What are you doing?
Kenneth	I'm talking hypothetically.
Sandra	Yes. I could go for someone younger yes.

Beat.

Kenneth	We're in love.
Sandra	I thought so.

Beat.

Kenneth	But something's gone wrong.
Sandra	No.
Kenneth	We live in Reading.
	Something's gone wrong.
Sandra	. . .
Kenneth	It's all house. Children. Work. We never wanted it like this. I'm not happy you're not happy so . . .

They look at each other. It's true.

Right.

Yes. There.

Sandra	. . .

Kenneth   Chris?

Sandra   . . .

Kenneth   Yes?

Sandra   We should get the kids down here it's nearly. . .

Kenneth   Sandra –

Sandra   Jamie!

Kenneth   Sandra I can see –

Sandra   Jamie! It's time.

Kenneth   I know what you've done why won't you admit /
it?

Sandra   Rosie, three minutes! Come down, we're doing
the cake! If I have Ken, if I had done something
as well, how would that help, if we'd both been
lying to each other what are you suggesting
we do?

Kenneth   Chris. Yes?

Sandra   Jesus Ken leave it / alone

Kenneth   I don't know what we do but at least we could
start with the truth. We were never like this, we
were honest.

Sandra   I'm getting the cake.

Kenneth   Chris.

Sandra   No.

Kenneth   Yes.

Sandra   NO!

Kenneth   Sandra

Sandra   Alright!

Yes. Fresh meat. Exactly. Four months. He's good. It helps.

Alright?

Kenneth   Yes.

Sandra   Good.

Now we're really in trouble.

Well done.

Jamie *enters.*

Sandra   Come and sit down Jamie, would you like some wine?

Jamie   What?

Kenneth   He's fourteen.

Jamie   Okay. Is this because it's Rosie's birthday?

Sandra   How about a cigarette?

Jamie   Mum . . .

Kenneth   Ignore her.

Sandra   He smokes anyway.

Jamie   No I don't.

Sandra   Oh come ON.

Jamie   I've had a –

Sandra   Just *take one.*

He looks at her. She's serious.

Jamie   Alright.

He does.

Got a lighter?

She gives him one, he lights it effortlessly.

Where's Rosie?

Sandra   I'm just going to get the cake.

She goes, shouting on her way.

Sandra   Rosie if you don't come down now there'll be trouble! We've made an effort for you don't want you sulking. I'll show her shouting.

ROSIE!

NOW!

She goes out.

Pause.

Jamie *and* **Kenneth** *look at each other.*

Jamie   Didn't know you smoked Dad.

Kenneth   Yeah.

Jamie   It suits you.

Kenneth   Thanks.

Beat.

You too.

Jamie   Thanks.

They smoke.

Rose *comes in, very unhappy. She sits.*

Jamie   Do you want a cigarette?

Rose   Shut up.

Silence.

They sit together.

Kenneth *checks his watch.*

Kenneth   Thirty seconds.

Silence.

Then from off:

Sandra   Happy birthday to you!

They all join in as **Sandra** *enters with the cake. Fifteen candles are lit. She puts it on the table.*

All apart from **Rose***.*

Happy birthday to you.

Happy birthday dear Rosie.

Happy birthday to you!

A moment. They look at **Rosie***.*

Sandra   Blow them out then.

She does.

They don't all go out.

She sits for a moment.

She's about to do the rest when **Jamie** *blows them out, with lots of smoke.*

Sandra   Oh.

Kenneth   Jamie!

Jamie   She didn't do it properly.

Sandra   Ahhh! My little boy smoking in front of his mother.

A proper family at last.

Cake everyone?

She divides up the cake.

Now as you might've heard, your father and I have been having a conversation, an adult conversation but since you're both grown up now in your own way tonight I think we should lay it out for you what do you think Ken?

Kenneth   No I don't think we should actually / Sandra.

Sandra   Your father went and found someone else and
                had sex with her. Her name was Frankie.

        Rose *looks at her dad.* **Jamie** *smokes.*

Sandra   She was young. It was revenge as he thought I
                was having an affair myself which if we're
                honest, if we're really laying this all out for you
                in the middle of the night, well . . . there's a man
                called Chris. Chris is not the sort of man you
                would expect me to be sleeping with, but it
                seems that both of us have felt in some way
                frustrated and we've found a way out – does
                everyone have a piece of cake?

        No one replies.

Kenneth   Can we talk about / this later –

Sandra   Now we still both love each other, don't worry
                about that. But we both feel trapped, we live, as
                you know, in Reading, and we never intended to
                be in this domestic situation we are both feeling
                that maybe human beings were not designed to
                be monogamous do you both know what that
                word means?

        Neither answers.

                We both feel that maybe sleeping around is our
                natural state, so that in itself might have been
                alright but the issue – and Ken do correct me –
                the issue is trust. We can't be lying to each other.
                That would be pointless.

                As you grow up, both of you, you'll learn that in
                love as everything else there is no such thing as a
                happy ending. We're animals.

                So the question we have is –

Rose   Why are you telling us this?

Sandra	Rosie I'm talking. Eat your cake. We're animals and what happens happens so the conclusion your father and I have come to is that we should get divorced that's right isn't it Ken? We didn't want to mention it to you until we were sure but having talked about it I think we've come to a joint decision now haven't we?
Kenneth	A divorce?
Sandra	I know it must be difficult, but it's the right thing.
Kenneth	Sandra SHUT / UP.
Rose	/ I don't want to hear THIS!
Sandra	It's really important we don't confuse our children and really a divorce is the only way forward.
Kenneth	It's what you want?
Sandra	The only way we can be free. And we always said –
Rose	Why are you telling us like this?
Sandra	It's not fair on the children us going at each other / all the time.
Rose	I asked a question.
Sandra	Ken, we've made a decision really haven't we, and we'll stay in touch. We'll still be friends.
Kenneth	I don't know.
Sandra	I think things are different now I think things have changed, we're entitled to do our own thing follow our own path, no one can tell us what's *right*, not church not the government, not even our children, it's no one's business but our own.

We've got our lives to live Ken, you, me, Rosie, Jamie, when it comes down to it we're all separate people these days. On our own paths.

There's a bit of you that's excited about this. Isn't there?

There's a little bit of you excited about the possibilities of striking out, on your own?

Kenneth   Yes.

A pause.

Sandra   So there we are children. Mum and Dad are going to be happier.

And trust me. You'll be happier too.

Rosie *suddenly gets up and leaves.*

A moment.

Kenneth   Why?

Sandra   Did you say something?

Kenneth   Why are you involving them?

Sandra   Because technically we're a family.

Look. Jamie's still here.

Jamie *is smoking and not looking at them.*

Sandra   He's pleased I've laid it all out.

He's pleased we're up front so he knows what's coming. They know about their parents. They're not children. He smokes. Rosie's doing all sorts of thing with her *boyfriend* I bet she's having a whale of a time.

Jamie   She's split up with him.

Kenneth   What?

Jamie   He slept with Sarah Franks last weekend. She's
              only just found out. That's what she was doing
              on the phone. Heard her crying. He doesn't
              want her anymore.

Sandra   Well . . .

              Proves my point.

              No happy endings.

A pause.

Rosie *screams from upstairs.*

Sandra   What was –

Jamie   It's Rosie.

Kenneth   She sounded –

Another scream. **Kenneth** *goes.*

Sandra *waits for a second, unsure, then goes after*
Kenneth.

Another scream. Sobbing.

From off:

Kenneth   Rosie!

Sandra   Rosie!

Kenneth   Are you alright? It's not important. What your
              mother was saying . . .

Sobbing. Banging. **Jamie** *lights another cigarette.*

Kenneth   Open the door Rosie.

A banging.

              Rosie!

More banging and shouting.

Jamie *goes and puts the tape back in.*

*She Bangs the Drums plays again – picking up from where
it left off.*

Jamie *sings along quietly.*

Underneath the banging and the shouting continues.

Jamie *gets the rest of the wine and drinks from the bottle.*

As the curtain falls and the lights fade the music mixes with the banging on the door.

In the dark just a thumping.

Interval.

Three

Thumping.

We hear Sexy Chick by David Guetta feat. Akon.

As the drums come in . . . curtain up to reveal . . .

2011. A living room in a large country house. French windows open out onto a large garden. Light pours in. An iPad is plugged into a dock – playing the music and the video to the song.

Rose *enters, with a bag, having come in the front door. She is now 37, lives in London, and is dressed in slightly old clothes.*

She looks around – where is everyone?

Jamie *enters through the French windows with his iPhone. He is 35, unshaven, and wearing a grey hooded top. He tips the iPhone around, playing Labyrinth intently. Doesn't look up. Nods in time with the music.*

He stops. Still doesn't look up.

Then she goes over and switches off the iPad. **Jamie** *turns round.*

Jamie	Oh.
	Rose *smiles.*
Rose	Hello.
	She goes over and hugs him.
Jamie	Aren't you coming tomorrow?
Rose	No.
Jamie	Dad said you were coming on Wednesday.
Rose	It is Wednesday.
Jamie	Oh.
	Have you seen this?
Rose	What?

Jamie	It's a game, you . . . you have to get the ball in the hole.
Rose	Right.
Jamie	You've got an iPhone though haven't you?
Rose	Yeah.
Jamie	You should download it then.
	He goes back to playing it.
Rose	How's things?
Jamie	Yeah good.
Rose	The job?
Jamie	Yeah it's alright. You know, it's you know it's flexible.
Rose	Been there a while now.
Jamie	What?
Rose	Been driving for them a while.
Jamie	Yeah six months or whatever.
Rose	You like it?
Jamie	Yeah yeah.
Rose	You still doing your course?
Jamie	What? No.
Rose	You . . .
Jamie	Didn't . . . teacher was shit.
Rose	Right.
Jamie	Giving it all – Didn't know what he was talking about. I was I was cleverer than him I could tell I was like, er have you have you thought of the social factor he didn't know what I what I was talking about I was like this guy's a fraud this guy doesn't know anything. I get bored quickly.

Rose	I know.
Jamie	Didn't like it so I stopped.
	Beat.
Rose	So what is it now?
Jamie	Gonna go travelling.
Rose	You said that before.
Jamie	Saving up.
Rose	Where?
Jamie	Australia. My My My friend – you remember – Kate.
Rose	You're still in touch with her.
Jamie	Yeah Facebook. Gonna go and stay with her, for a bit.
Rose	Right.
Jamie	Supposed to be mental out there.
Rose	Right.
	Mental.
Jamie	Yeah.
	Beat.
Rose	How's Dad?
Jamie	Alright.
Rose	Must be around the house a bit more now.
Jamie	Yeah.
Rose	Annoying is it?
Jamie	No it's good. He picks me up.
Rose	What?
Jamie	From the pub.

Rose   Right.

Jamie   We get on so. Yeah. Can be annoying but you but you. You get used to it.

Rose   Right. Jamie?

Jamie   What?

Rose   Can you stop playing that for a minute?

Jamie   What? Oh . . . what? Is it, is it? I'm not being rude.

Rose   I haven't seen you in months.

Jamie   I'm not being rude. Don't get annoyed.

          She sighs.

          Don't get annoyed with me.

Rose   I'm asking you Jamie.

Jamie   Right, right. Hang on.

          Pause.

          He stops.

          Puts it away, walks around a bit.

Jamie   What then? What do you want then?

Rose   Nothing, just . . . do you want a cup of tea?

Jamie   Nah I'm alright.

          Beat.

Rose   What happened with the flat?

Jamie   What? Oh.

Rose   Last time I was here you were trying to find somewhere.

Jamie   Too expensive it's like I could spend all my money on the rent you know or I can live here and have money no contest and as I as I said Dad's cool, he's like a mate, but I don't have to

Rose	Don't have to pay rent.
Jamie	Yeah exactly. It's expensive. Costs loads.
Rose	I know.
Jamie	Yeah. Do you rent?
Rose	Of course.
Jamie	Yeah right so you so you know.
Rose	It's more expensive in London.
Jamie	I couldn't live in London. I went there the other day, we went there went there to see a play.
Rose	What?
Jamie	*Wicked*.
Rose	That's a musical.
Jamic	Ycah it was good, but wc wcnt to thc pub and it was like five quid for a pint and we were we were like I said I said I think there's a mistake you're charging us five quid and the guy – everyone in London's rude you know? You know?
Rose	Who did you go with?
Jamie	What?
Rose	To see *Wicked*.
Jamie	Dad.
Rose	You didn't say.
Jamie	What?
Rose	I'm in London. You didn't call I could've met you.
Jamie	Didn't . . . what? Didn't think of it. So. What? Shit. Don't get annoyed with me yeah?
Rose	I'm not.

Jamie	What is this?
Rose	No.
Jamie	Sounds like you you were so so
Rose	It doesn't matter, I'm glad you liked the show.
Jamie	Yeah it was good. Interval, it was good it had an interval you can go out have a smoke.
Rose	Right.
	Where's Dad?
Jamie	Out there?
Rose	What?
Jamie	The garden. I'll get him.

Suddenly **Jamie** *goes out the French windows.*

Rose *is left on her own.*

She looks around.

The house is beautiful.

Expensive equipment, art, ornaments. Perfect.

She goes to the wall.

Touches it.

Leans on it. Something's wrong.

Kenneth *enters through the French windows. He is now 64, and wears a shirt, white flannel trousers. He has gained a bit of weight, but is still looking healthy.* **Jamie** *follows behind him.*

Kenneth	My favourite daughter.
Rose	Your only daughter.
Kenneth	This is true. Sharp as a button.
Rose	Buttons aren't sharp.
Kenneth	I meant bright.

Rose	I think you did.
Kenneth	Bright as a button.
Rose	There you are.
Kenneth	My favourite daughter.

He goes and kisses and hugs her.

How was the train?

Rose	Fine.
Kenneth	You didn't want to drive?
Rose	Got rid of my car.
Kenneth	Oh right.
Rose	Ages ago.
Kenneth	Suppose it's not worth it in London?
Rose	Well . . .
Kenneth	And the train was alright?
Rose	Yeah.
Kenneth	I can't stand them, not these days. Do you want a drink?
Rose	I'm alright thanks. Got water.
Kenneth	We're on the white wine. Aren't we Jamie?
Jamie	Yeah. Yeah.
Kenneth	Colin got back from France on Monday. You know Colin?
Rose	No.
Kenneth	Plays golf, he went on a bit of booze cruise, we put in an order didn't we?
Jamie	Yeah.
Kenneth	And here are the fruits, of his labour, bottled up, he went for quality, all the way to the south and

you really can taste the difference, if you'll
pardon the expression. Sit down sit down.

They do.

So.

Exciting.

Rose   What?

Kenneth   Your news.

Rose   It's not news.

Kenneth   The 'summit'.

Rose   Yeah

Kenneth   I loved it, calling us up, 'I want us all to meet'.

Rose   Right.

Kenneth   'I want us all to be in the same place for once.'

Rose

Kenneth   'I have something to say'

Rose   Yeah.

Kenneth   It's good. It's a good excuse – haven't seen your
              mother in months.

Rose   Henry's funeral.

Kenneth   Right. Yes, right. I suppose so. Did you see her?

Rose   What?

Kenneth   At the funeral. The party after. Did you see what
              she was up to?

Rose   No.

Kenneth   Flirting with the waiter. While Clive was right
              there. Right in his face, there she was, flirting
              away with this Greek bloke.

Rose   She was drunk.

Kenneth   That's what she's like.

Rose   Yes.

Kenneth   Uncontrollable.

Rose   Uncontrollable.

Kenneth   Got to admire her really.

Rose   . . .

Pause.

Kenneth   You alright love?

Rose   . . .

Beat.

Kenneth   Jamie's still got his job.

Rose   Yeah I know. He said.

It's good.

Kenneth   Yeah.

They're both looking at **Jamie**, *who's not been listening.*

Jamie   What?

Kenneth   How's the flat?

Rose   Fine.

Kenneth   And Sarah?

Rose   What?

Kenneth   It is Sarah? Your flatmate.

Rose   She moved out last year.

Kenneth   Oh right, who is it now then?

Rose   This bloke Paul.

Kenneth   A bloke – what does Andrew make of that?
– who's Paul?

Rose   Some guy from Gumtree.

Kenneth   Gumtree?

Rose   You advertise on it if you've got a room going.

Kenneth   So Paul's really just some bloke?

Rose   Yeah.

Kenneth   Is that. That's. . .

Rose   What?

Kenneth   You're happy with that are you?

Rose   Not really.

Kenneth   Wouldn't have been allowed when I was your age, sharing – man and a women. Together like that, would've been an outrage. A sin.

Rose   Well the rent needs paying.

Beat.

Kenneth   You know if you need any help with anything.

Rose   Yeah.

Kenneth   Good good.

Suddenly **Jamie** *unzips his hoody, takes off his T-shirt and strides out into the sun of the garden.*

Kenneth   He's off then.

Beat.

Rose   Is he alright?

Kenneth   What do you mean?

Rose   He seems worse.

Kenneth   Don't know what you mean.

Rose   The repeating. The – he's going round in circles.

Kenneth   Rosie, you always say this, I think it's cruel.

Rose   He used to be bright.

Kenneth   He's his own person. He's very intelligent.

Rose   But he's not Dad. He really isn't. Not anymore.

Kenneth   He's just – he doesn't fit in to what people want. But he's wonderful. When he had that thing in the centre with the disabled kids.

Rose   He never turned up.

Kenneth   It was early mornings, but when he was there he was brilliant. Why do you want to get at him?

Rose   I just wonder if he should . . . get help or something.

Kenneth   Leave him alone. He's happy.

Rose   But that's not –

Kenneth   What?

Beat.

Rose   Nothing.

Kenneth   Are you alright?

   Rose *turns away.*

   A strange moment.

   Then she turns back.

Rose   How's retirement?

Kenneth   I don't know why I didn't do it before. Times my own. Me and Jamie we do the garden, he likes it, then we go to the pub. It's bliss. Golf. Perfect.

Rose   Good.

Kenneth   You know I worked out with the pension and the payments, and the income from the Birmingham house, I'm making over sixty thousand a year.

Rose   Right.

Kenneth	Not bad for doing nothing.
Rose	Yeah.
Kenneth	And I mean now you're all out of university or whatever, and everything's paid off so the money's my own. Good isn't it?
Rose	Yeah.
Kenneth	Life of luxury.
Rose	Sixty thousand.
Kenneth	Yep.
Rose	Almost three times what I make now.
Kenneth	What? No. Is it?
Rose	Yeah, and I'm working all the time.
Kenneth	Really?
Rose	. . .
Kenneth	Well at least you're doing what you want to do aren't you?
Rose	. . .

A doorbell.

Kenneth	Who's –
Rose	Mum.
Kenneth	Can't be. She's supposed to be here at two.
Rose	Its half past.
Kenneth	Oh. Is it? Wonderful.

He goes out.

Rose *nearly cries, but stops herself.*

Voices off stage.

Sandra	You've done something to the front?

Kenneth	Landscaped the drive.
Sandra	Looks cheap.
Kenneth	My choice.
Sandra	Just saying Kenneth, no need / to snap at me.
Kenneth	I know, I know you're always / just saying.
Sandra	Is she here?
Kenneth	She's in a mood.
Sandra	Oh good, just how I like to spend a sunny day, dealing with one of Rosie's *moods*.
Kenneth	Be careful.
Sandra	I'm always careful. Through here?

They enter. **Sandra** *is now 64, dressed expensively and tastefully for the occasion and the weather. Her skin is amazing. She has looked after herself.*

Sandra	Hello!
Rose	Hi Mum.

She goes and kisses and hugs her.

Sandra	I remember this baby. Look at you. I don't see you enough.
Rose	It's good you're here.
Sandra	Well you called and here I am. Here we both are, your father and your mother together again isn't it something? You look healthy.
Rose	What does that mean?
Sandra	Healthy. Healthy. Not ill. Healthy. What do you think it means?
Rose	Fat?
Sandra	Don't be silly you're not fat, why haven't you got a drink?

Rose	I don't want one.
Sandra	Diet.
Rose	No.
Sandra	Pregnant?
Rose	No.
Sandra	Because you've called us all together to tell us something and now you're not drinking.
Rose	I'm not pregnant.
Sandra	You're sure?
Rose	Mum –
Sandra	I was convinced that's what this was about, well never mind, I know I could do with a drink.
Kenneth	We're on the wine.
Sandra	Are you? You never had any taste for wine. Your dad, Rosie, he never had any taste for anything, except women – he didn't do too badly there.
Kenneth	I'll get you a glass.
Sandra	That's an idea, and music, I suppose he knew a thing or two about his music. Come on sit down then. How are you? Not pregnant we know that. How's it going?
Rose	Good.
Sandra	How are the gigs?
Rose	On and off.
Sandra	I loved it at Christmas.
Rose	Yeah it was good you came.
Sandra	I loved it. We both enjoyed it.
Rose	How's Clive?
Sandra	Not well.

Rose   Right.

Sandra   But we ply him with booze and it does the trick. Doctor says it won't help but I think Clive's long past that, and we say will it actually kill him? All the booze and doctor says not immediately so off we go, gin, sherry, this whisky we got from Islay. You've not been to Islay have you Ken?

Kenneth   I haven't had the pleasure no.

He gives her some wine.

There you are.

Sandra   Well you should. Why don't you go with Kerry?

Kenneth   Not with Kerry anymore.

Rose   They split up.

Sandra   What?

Kenneth   I split up with Kerry months ago.

Sandra   Why?

Kenneth *shrugs.*

Sandra   You're such a *man* Ken, look at him. You should update me. Put it on Facebook. I'm on Facebook now. I love it. Ken you should join now you're single.

Kenneth   Jamie tried to set me up but it's all nonsense really isn't it? Poking and walls and everything else.

Sandra   Baby I looked you up, why aren't you on it?

Rose   I was.

Sandra   All your friends are. You were? What happened?

Rose   I deleted my account.

Sandra   Why?

Rose   . . .

Sandra	Well I love it. Photos, all of that. It's good for flirting too and Clive doesn't understand computers won't go near one, so it's entirely safe. You know you can actually chat to people on it? I love it. This wine isn't bad Ken.
Kenneth	Told you.
Sandra	Where's it from?
Kenneth	France. Got twenty bottles in the garage. You can take one with you.
Sandra	You can give me a couple when I go.
Kenneth	I just said that.
Sandra	What?
Kenneth	I'll give you a case.
Sandra	Lovely. This isn't bad. Where's Jamie?
Rose	Sunbathing.
Sandra	He knows what's good for him. Bless him.
Kenneth	Shall I . . .
Sandra	No don't disturb him wouldn't get any sense out of him anyway, away with the fairies, see him later. Shall we get started then? Get it over and done with Rose? Very exciting.
	Isn't it?
	You want to talk to us.
Rose	Dad can you sit down?
Kenneth	Oh right.
Sandra	He's always the same isn't he? No attention span. Look at him.
Kenneth	I just can't concentrate any more. No need to. I love it. Freedom! At last!

Sandra	Your father, still all over the place. Come on Ken. Sit down. She's getting annoyed. She wants us all to *talk*.
Rose	I'm not annoyed.
Sandra	See?

He sits down.

Kenneth	I have now sat down.
Sandra	Alright then love.
	All yours. Off you go.
Rose	Don't . . .
Sandra	What?
Rose	Don't patronise me.
Sandra	What?
Rose	I'm not a kid.
Sandra	I know. We all know that. What a strange thing to say.
	Of course you're not.
Rose	
Sandra	I'm just saying, I'm here for you. We're listening. Gosh.
Kenneth	Let her speak.
Sandra	I am. That's what I'm doing. I'm prompting.
	Speak.
	Go on love.

Pause.

Rose	I want you to buy me a house.

Sandra *smiles.*

Kenneth *laughs.*

Sandra   A house?

       Kenneth *laughs some more.*

Kenneth   You've got a house.

Rose   I'm renting.

Kenneth   Your flat.

Rose   I rent it.

Kenneth   Thought you liked it.

Rose   I . . . No.

      . . . I . . .

      Oh.

Kenneth   What's the matter love?

Sandra   Something's wrong isn't it? I can tell.

      Rose *laughs.*

Rose   Yeah one or two things yeah one or two things have gone a bit wrong.

Sandra   Come on then.

Kenneth   We've got nothing else to do this afternoon love.

Rose   Don't get drunk.

Sandra   I've only just arrived. Look as I said we're here for you, but we don't need to be insulted.

      Yes?

      We're well past that. Aren't we Ken? We can do without.

      Yes?

      Let's make that clear.

Kenneth   We won't get drunk love.

      Pause. **Rosie** *gathers herself again.*

Rose	I'm thirty-seven.
Sandra	Yes we know. My baby.
Rose	It was my birthday, in March.
Sandra	We sent you a card. Didn't we? Clive and I did anyway, Kenneth did you?
Rose	Mum!
Kenneth	Course I / sent her a card
Rose	Shut up yeah?
Sandra	Okay, alright, we've been having fun, having a good time up till now but maybe it's not clear Rosie I don't have to be shouted at, you understand? We could all be doing lots of / other things –
Rose	Do what you like.
Sandra	Just carry on.
Rose	So . . . my birthday. I had a little thing in a bar in Clapham, hired out this little bar, and all my friends came, and two days before I didn't tell you this, but *two days* before my birthday I broke up with Andy.
Kenneth	You didn't . . . oh . . . you're not with.
Rose	No.
Kenneth	You didn't say.
Rose	You never asked.
Sandra	You don't like us asking.
Rose	Yeah so I'd already booked this bar, and I went ahead with it anyway even though I was quite . . . *lonely* . . . you know.
Sandra	Oh baby.

Rose	And everyone turned up and some of them with kids and stuff and we had a bit of a dance you know, kept the smiles going but then suddenly I found I was sat on a chair at the side of the room, all on my own, at my own party, and I was crying.
Sandra	Were you drinking gin?
Rose	No.
Sandra	Gin can do that.
Rose	I wasn't drinking at all Mum but I found I was crying, and it was because I realised as I was sat there, I realised I'd completely fucked it up.
Sandra	What?
Rose	I . . . thought I'm thirty-seven and I've had a good time in London, sort of – but what have I got? No flat, no kids, no partner, no car, ten thousand in unsecured debt.
Sandra	You're doing what you wanted darling, not many people can –
Rose	What I wanted at seventeen but I'm nearly forty and I've got nothing.
	And I was sat there at the side of the room and I thought where did it go wrong? And walking down the street it hit me and the more I thought about it the more obvious it was.
	It's your fault. All of it.
	I wanted to tell you, I thought you should know.
Kenneth	Our fault.
Sandra	Baby.
Kenneth	Our fault. / I see.

Sandra	You're upset I understand, you're obviously in some kind of state we can see that but don't turn this at us, you're being ridiculous. / We've given you everything –
Rose	Don't get *offended*. Listen to me.
Sandra	Well you're accusing us of –
Rose	I've done everything / I was told to do.
Sandra	Just stood there and accusing us of ruining your life, this melodramatic streak / it comes from your father.
Rose	I worked hard at school, / got my results.
Kenneth	What's that suppose to mean?
Rose	You said go to university to get a job so that's what I did, but when I came out there weren't any jobs.
Sandra	A degree was something to fall back on.
Rose	A degree means nothing.
Sandra	Well you didn't need it in the end anyway you –
Rose	Yeah right exactly, as you said I should, as you *encouraged* me to do, I followed my dream, did what you said was *important*, following my *passion*.
Sandra	You're really talking look at her Ken.
Kenneth	I am
Rose	I didn't settle down too early, didn't compromise and I *thought* I really believed, because you *told me* Mum, you *assured* me, that a woman can have it all, you were my example.
Sandra	I'll take / that as a compliment –

Rose	– you said, as did everyone else, there's no hurry to have kids these days, so I waited until I had built up my career, but the problem was my career never happened.
Kenneth	You weren't to know how / things would turn out.
Rose	Well I was to know,
Sandra	You've done alright.
Rose	I was to know for a simple reason which is that *I'm not very good*. But you always encouraged me. Everyone did, my teachers, you, the college, all of them said I should keep going when obviously, looking back, *clearly* –
Kenneth	It's just difficult, it's a difficult / profession –
Rose	Everyone knew. All the time, you knew I wasn't great, but out of *kindness*, you didn't say and instead just watched me entirely fuck up waste my life away.
Sandra	
Rose	All my friends who got proper boring jobs have a brilliant time – for fifteen years they've been able to afford parties, drinks, holidays while I'm still temping between gigs, and then they had babies but I waited, I was working too much, too hard, with music, this *hobby*, but now I'm old, really old. You know where Andy's gone?
Sandra	Look –
Kenneth	Andy? What do you mean?
Rose	She's twenty-four and desperate for kids. That's where he's gone.
	To her. She doesn't want a career.
	So where does that leave me?

Kenneth   Love –

Rose   Stuck on the bottom fucking shelf.

    Beat.

Kenneth   You said it was what you wanted.

Rose   I needed guidance, real honest guidance when I was young – perspective, but instead you let me, you encouraged me to –

Sandra   Is this getting to a point darling?

Rose   Yes it's getting to a *point*.

Sandra   Because it sounds like a moan.

Rose   Well sorry for taking up your time Mum.

Sandra   I can think of better ways to spend my afternoon.

Rose   Granny and Granddad lived through the war, lived through rations, their lot built the welfare state. They *worked* hard.

Kenneth   We've worked hard. Forty years, both of us, every day –

Rose   And what have you lot done? Climbed the ladder and broke it as you went.

Sandra   Kenneth top me up. This is good stuff.

    He does.

Rose   You got your cheap flights and your nice cars but never looked at what they were doing to the environment, you voted in Thatcher, destroyed the unions, reduced taxes,

Sandra   / Politics!

Rose   Tony fucking Blair, now surprise surprise you've voted in the Tories again. All because you want to cling on to your money but here I am, your

own daughter, and I can't afford a house, a car
– a child.

Sandra   It's not too late, you're not even forty.

Rose   At my age you had a house, half paid off, two
kids, holidays, money.

Kenneth   It was different then.

Sandra   That's right, completely different.

Rose   Look at you . . . 'If you can remember the sixties
you weren't really there'. What a smug fucking
little thing to say. You didn't change the world,
you bought it. Privatised it. What did you stand
for? Peace? Love? Nothing except being able to
do whatever the fuck you wanted.

Sandra   What about our divorce you haven't mentioned
that yet, I'd bring that in if I were you.

Rose   Yeah okay – right, Granny and Granddad made
an effort. To stay together. For you. But you just
. . . one night. Over. Done. Not even what
happened to me made you think about it. You
still said you didn't want to be trapped. It's not a
trap, it's called responsibility. I don't think Jamie
ever got over it all falling apart.

Kenneth   Jamie's fine actually. Jamie's perfectly happy. It's
you I'm worried about now.

Sandra   So *dramatic*.

Rose   It was dramatic. To me. To both of us. At the
time. It was a big fucking deal. I promise you.

Sandra   You must be exhausted.

Are we having lunch? Or do you want to get to
the point?

Rose   My point is you should buy me a house.

Kenneth   Why?

Rose	What?
Kenneth	Why should we buy you a house?
Sandra	We can't afford it love. Either of us.
Kenneth	But even if we could. I'm sorry Rosie, you know we love you, you know we'd do almost anything for you, but there has to come a day when you live your life.
	Most of what you're saying has nothing to do with us.
	As you said you're nearly forty. You've had opportunities. You've made choices.
	Better or worse. No one made you play the violin.
	No one made you keep going.
Rose	But you always said what a shame it would be –
Kenneth	Why did you listen to us?
	We're your parents.
	Sandra and me, we never listened to a word our parents said.
	Why the hell did you take any notice of what we told you?
	You're supposed to rebel.
	That's what you're supposed to do.
Sandra	I remember telling my mum to fuck off.
	I was seventeen. It was the best moment of my life.
	Love, you've never told me to fuck off have you?
Rose	Yes.
Sandra	No.

Rose   You don't hear me.

Sandra   Well then that's the problem.

              Isn't it?

Rose   Mum?

Sandra   Darling.

Rose   Fuck off.

Beat.

Kenneth   It's your life Rosie.

              It has to be.

He drinks from the wine.

              We love you.

              But you can't blame us.

              You want us to give up our retirement, our
              independence, our holidays, our security as we
              get older, you want to take all of that away from
              us and just *give* you a house.

Rose   It's not fair.

Kenneth   Life isn't.

Rose   . . .

Kenneth   I'm surprised you don't know that by now.

Rose   . . .

Sandra

Kenneth   Isn't your mother quiet?

              Beat.

              Look, why don't you have a glass of wine and
              we'll –

Sandra	At least your father and me we never went crawling back to our parents.
Kenneth	Alright Sandra –
Rose	I'm not crawling
Sandra	Looks like it to me –
Kenneth	Sandra –
Sandra	I'm a woman, you don't know what I faced for thirty years every place I went to work, we didn't just climb the ladder women like me, we made it, we built it all, you don't understand the world as it was Rosie, I'm sorry but you have no idea –
Rose	It's not just me. Everyone I know has less than their parents did at their age. They're bringing their children up in these little houses, these tiny flats, the best they can afford, while their parents sit on all the money, in huge houses, with big empty rooms. It's disgusting.
Sandra	It's not all about money.
Rose	YES IT IS! IT IS *ALL* ABOUT FUCKING MONEY.
Sandra	I pity you. If that's what you think Rosie. I really pity you.
Rose	Mum. It's simple. Buy me a house.
	You can.
	Either of you could.
	Please.
Sandra	What's this really about?
	Darling?
Rose	You're supposed to look after your children.

Jamie *comes in.*

Jamie   What's going on? I don't I don't . . . I can't . . . I'm getting a headache! The SHOUTING! I'm trying to relax. I can't I can't – I can't I can't –

Sandra   Jamie –

She goes to him, but he deliberately moves away from her, nearer to **Rosie** *and* **Kenneth**.

Rose   Come on Jamie. Jamie, it's alright. We'll go into the garden.

Jamie   What?

Rose   Go for a walk. You can have a smoke. Or, whatever. We'll catch up yeah.

Jamie   Yeah, right. Yeah.

He looks at her, trusts her. **Jamie** *exits.*

Rose   Dad?

               Dad.

               You understand.

               . . . ?

He looks at her, hard.

Kenneth   No.

She goes.

Sandra   I thought our children would be heroes.

               I imagined they would soar. Standing on our shoulders I assumed that our kids would reach heights we never imagined, change the world entirely. I thought they would solve the great problems become prime ministers, scientists, academics.

               But look at them. They sit on computers, not living, typing messages about nothing. Watching meaningless videos, and waiting for Friday night, they want to be rich and famous, in fact that's all they want to be, but they never lift a fucking finger.

Do they?

They don't read, they don't work and they don't *think*. They want it all on a plate.

And then strangely when nothing arrives, it's our fault.

What happened?

I thought you're supposed to be proud of your children.

Can we buy her a house?

But no, NO! you're right – Sometimes I go into the garden, you've seen our garden, I go out there and lie on the grass, and I think I haven't done this since I was young. For forty years it's been hard graft. We've worked ourselves to the bone.

Pause.

Top me up Ken.

He does.

Sandra   Maybe it was me.

Kenneth   No.

Sandra   I've got a mouth like a train, you know that, I'm a very confident person, maybe I was overbearing.

Kenneth   We never went to bed with an argument still hanging. They weren't unhappy growing up.

Sandra   Our daughter slit her wrists.

Kenneth

Sandra   I still think of it.

I dream of the blood. On the floor.

She might do it again, I still see her as a little girl.

Kenneth   She'll be alright.

Sandra   I don't know Ken we've been saying that for twenty years, don't worry, she'll be alright but now she's here saying what she's saying and she's nearly forty and I'm starting to think maybe she's got a point.

Maybe she won't be . . .

Alright.

Maybe she has wasted her life.

As you said. It isn't fair.

Perhaps we just got lucky.

Pause.

They drink the wine.

Kenneth   Have you got a fag?

Sandra   Ken! You don't.

Ken   Well.

Sandra   Not for years.

Ken   Well

They get out cigarettes.

He lights one. Then gives it to her.

He smiles and lights one himself.

A pause.

They take in the room.

Sandra   What do we do?

Kenneth   She knows we love her.

    Beat.

    She'll calm down, come back.

    Beat.

    She always does.

    Pause.

    You alright?

Sandra

    They smoke.

Sandra   What happened with you and Kerry?

Kenneth   She wasn't on my intellectual level.

Sandra   She was fat.

Kenneth   Thank you.

Sandra   Well she was you know as well I do she was rather overweight.

    He smiles.

Kenneth   You look great.

Sandra   Got a gym at home now. Every day, hour in the gym, pilates, pool.

Kenneth   Got a pool here.

Sandra   I know.

Kenneth   I could build a gym too.

Sandra   What?

Kenneth   Just saying.

Sandra   I know you.

Kenneth   You do.

Sandra   Never just saying. You could *build a gym*.

Kenneth   Well I could.

Sandra   What do you mean?

He looks at her.

Kenneth   You don't like Clive.

Sandra   I . . .

Kenneth   Come on.

He's fun but –

You don't like him really.

Do you?

She smiles.

He smiles.

A connection.

I want to die with you.

Sandra   That's a big thing to say.

Kenneth   I've always said big things.

Sandra   You stop me in my tracks sometimes Kenneth.

They look at each other.

Sometimes I don't think you'll ever end.

The way you look.

You're still –

Your eyes are bright.

They stare at each other.

Kenneth   Do you miss me?

Sandra   Clive doesn't dance.

Kenneth   Why not?

Sandra   His feet.

Kenneth   Never stopped me

Sandra   No. Medically. He has sores.

　　　　　Beat.

Kenneth   We never travelled.

Sandra   Our fair share.

Kenneth   I mean the world.

Sandra   Right.

Kenneth   We never saw the world together.

Sandra   No.

Kenneth   I'm retired now.

Sandra   So I hear.

Kenneth   You could leave Clive with a bottle of booze and a nurse. He won't know the difference.

Sandra

Kenneth   I'll sell this place, and off we go, you and me, world tour, whatever we want.

Sandra   What about Rosie?

　　　　　If we did that, if we spent all our money like that what would she . . .

　　　　　What sort of people would that make us?

Kenneth   We've worked hard.

Sandra   Yes but . . .

　　　　　He stands and goes to a cupboard.

　　　　　He looks through his records.

Sandra   What are you doing?

　　　　　Ken?

　　　　　What are you up to, burrowing around down there?

Ken!

Ken!

He finds a record and puts it on.

'All You Need Is Love' plays.

Sandra   Oh no.

Kenneth   You can dance to this.

Sandra   I'm married.

Kenneth   I thought you were the sort of girl that did what
she wanted.

Sandra   Ken –

Kenneth   Henry said you were a goer.

The song plays.

She stands up and goes towards him.

Sandra   Henry knew a good thing when he saw it.

They dance, as before.

It's kind of beautiful, with the sun, and the smoke.

They kiss.

Rose *enters, looks at them.*

Rose   Fuck's sake.

I thought you were divorced.

They smile, turn and look at her, warm – loving.

Rose *cries, then picks up her bag and storms out towards
the front door.* **Kenneth** *and* **Sandra** *keep on dancing.*

Jamie *walks in, sees the smoke and then goes to* **Sandra**'s
*packet of cigarettes, lights one, stands just outside the door,
and looks at the sky as he smokes.*

Rose *comes back in.*

Rose   Okay. I need a lift, to the station.

Can one of you give me a lift?

Mum.

Dad?

Mum.

Dad.

Mum.

Dad.

As the music descends in chaos, fade to black.

Curtain down.

Music continues to madness.

End.